Cici

Cici lives in a bayside suburb of Melbourne with her husband, Mike, and two kelpies. She has consciously followed a spiritual journey for the past 20 years. Her work has followed her passion which has led her on a path of self-enquiry. Cici founded a charity foundation where she served in a voluntary capacity as a director for 13 years providing support for people living with cancer and their families. She has run her own business for many years and been employed in hospital, community and clinical settings primarily in palliative care. Initially as an oncology massage therapist, a project officer in cancer services and health promotion co-ordinator, and then, as a pastoral carer/interfaith minister embracing diversity, equality and inclusion. More recently, she has been working as a bereavement counsellor and group facilitator. The decision to walk a spiritual pilgrimage was her next step in continuing to live a passionate life.

Mike

Starting his career as a banking lawyer, Mike left the legal profession to build a business in workplace investigations and dispute resolution before burning out and retreating to the Mornington Peninsula in Victoria with his wife and two dogs to take stock. In midlife, he began to make choices about who he wanted to be and what he wanted to do – the opportunity to do the Camino came along, and deepened his search for meaningful work and adventure. He now has a renewed focus where he works with workplaces to maintain mental health and create healthy cultures.

For Shirley, who waited for us to return but could not hold on long enough. For David, a warm and open-hearted friend and *peregrino*. You are much remembered and sadly missed.

Cici Edwards-Jensen And Mike Jensen

HAPPINESS IS THAT WAY

55 DAYS ON THE CAMINO VIA DE LA PLATA

AUSTIN MACAULEY PUBLISHERS™

LONDON * CAMBRIDGE * NEW YORK * SHARJAH

A CIP catalogue record for this title is available from the British Library.

ISBN 9781398411951 (Paperback)
ISBN 9781398411968 (ePub e-book)

www.austinmacauley.com

First Published 2023
Austin Macauley Publishers Ltd®
1 Canada Square
Canary Wharf
London
E14 5AA

It was never our intention to write a book of our experience on the Camino. When we couldn't find a book on the Via de la Plata, our friends encouraged us to write one ourselves, describing in particular our very personal experiences, unlike books that describe factual details such as towns, distances, directions, places to stay, etc. We are so grateful to those who, on our return, listened with great curiosity and asked questions and who inspired us to put our story into print.

As novice pilgrims on our first Camino we had no idea what to expect along the way. We were heartened by the kindness and openness of the Spanish people in general; the friendliness and hospitality of the owners of cafés and restaurants such as Restaurante DP in Monesterio, Bar Grimaldo in Grimaldo, and El Mona in Villanueva de las Peras; the generosity of heart of the people who ran the albergues and who understood our quest; and the *peregrinos* we met and connected with who were an inspiration to us and are now lifelong friends. We feel truly blessed to have them in our lives.

It takes a team to bring a book to life – once we started, this project quickly took on a life of its own, at times consuming our lives and our weekends.

We would like to thank Kerryn Burgess, our editor, who was extremely thorough in checking the background of our manuscript. We value the relationship very much.

A big thank you to Madeleine Kane, who designed our book cover so creatively. Madeleine was a joy to work with.

Thank you to Jane Green of Everlasting Magic Design for her advice, guidance and ongoing support over the years.

Our printer, Chris Giacomi of Design to Print Solutions, came into our lives many years ago when we founded our charity foundation. He has been an ongoing professional presence. Thank you, Chris, for your ability to listen and to understand. Thank you also to Rosie for your attentiveness to our needs in formatting the pages.

We welcomed the expertise of Denise Taylor, our proof reader, who was so efficient and thorough and gave us further confidence to present our manuscript to the printer.

Finally, thank you to our family, friends and colleagues who continued to motivate us in varying ways on this writing journey, often asking us, 'What section are you working on at the moment?', 'How's it going?', 'What, still?', 'So when is the book coming out?' etc. etc. Thank you for the friendly prompts and nudges.

Buen Camino, amigos!

Table of Contents

Note to Reader

This book is a memoir of our impressions, thoughts and feelings on the Camino Vía de la Plata.

It is not intended to be a guidebook for the novice pilgrim who is embarking on this Camino. It does not identify or include all the villages, distances between towns and descriptions of the terrain along the way.

Should you like a guidebook, we are more than happy for you to contact us on: Happinessisthatway@gmail.com for suggestions on different authors and/or titles.

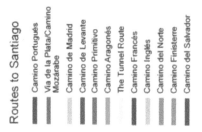

Routes to Santiago

- Camino Portugués
- Vía de la Plata/Camino Mozárabe
- Camino de Madrid
- Camino de Levante
- Camino Primitivo
- Camino Aragonés
- The Tunnel Route
- Camino Francés
- Camino Inglés
- Camino del Norte
- Camino Finisterre
- Camino del Salvador

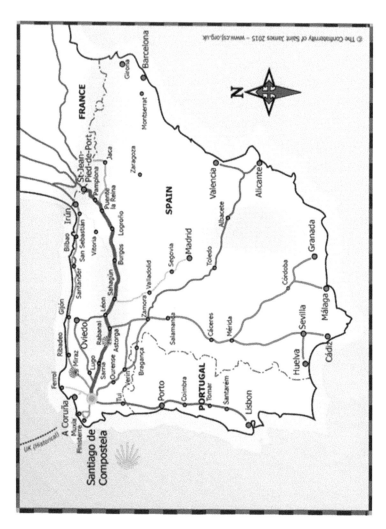

We would like to acknowledge the Confraternity of St James

Prelude

The scallop shell bears witness
To each footstep faithfully trodden
My badge of belonging
A seal of courage
Honouring my childlike innocence
Protector of my fearless heart and soul

– Cici Edwards-Jensen

Cici

All I can hear is my laboured breathing and the crunching of stones beneath my feet. The heat is unbearable. *Just focus on the horizon,* I keep thinking, *one foot in front of the other.* Heat stress is going to be my companion for some time. We have waited until October to begin our 1006 kilometre walk on the Vía de la Plata to avoid exactly this situation, yet today, on day one, the mercury has hit 35 degrees Celsius and there is no shade in sight.

The morning seems a lifetime ago. We left our hotel at six o'clock to walk to our starting point on the outskirts of Seville. In the cool morning air, Mike filmed me explaining what we were about to embark on and then we headed off in the dark with a spring in our step, our head torches shining into the unknown. Half an hour later, under a bridge next to a highway, we were lost. My backpack weighed heavily and I wondered how I had ever thought I would be able to carry it.

'Mike, we need to go back. Wait for the shops to open and buy a pram to push this stuff through Spain.'

I was serious. My dream of walking an authentic spiritual pilgrimage would be lost, along with all my credibility as a pilgrim, and I would be laughed out of Spain. None of my training came to mind, only feelings of being overwhelmed and unprepared. Then I thought of Reece Witherspoon hiking from California to

Oregon in the film *Wild*. My pack wasn't nearly as big as hers. If she could cope with walking with her elephant-sized pack, then I could do this.

Another half an hour later, we found our way onto the dirt track of the actual Camino. What a relief and what a great feeling to finally have our feet on the path. But now I am due for a pit stop. Squatting by the side of the road, I feel poised and balanced, proud that all those Pilates classes are kicking in. Well, almost. I haven't taken the weight of my pack into account, and suddenly I overbalance and go crashing backwards into a ditch. Thank goodness it is still dark and I don't lose every shred of dignity. I pray that I haven't shattered the scallop shell tied to the back of my pack. If that first hour was any indication of what lies ahead, life is going to get more than interesting.

Mike

It is still dark and we cannot see the stars for the amber lights from the city ring-road. Our conversation conceals our nervousness.

'You good?'

'Yep.'

'You? You good?'

'I think so.'

'You know where we're going?'

'Yep. Just get to the end of this bit and then there should be a yellow arrow…'

[pause]

'You good?'

It's almost impossible to spot these yellow arrows in the dark with the narrow beam of our head torches. We walk and scan from side to side with our lights, hoping not to miss an arrow that may indicate a sharp right or left turn. The packs take our concentration away from the path. We need to adjust them while we walk, which is strange, because we practised carrying them back home. They seem to have acquired extra weight since we left Melbourne. Already the straps are cutting into our shoulders, and it has been about half an hour since we saw a reassuring arrow. We double back a few times and question ourselves.

'Is this it?'

'Does this feel right to you?'

'I don't know…'

We arrive under a bridge where there are discarded mattresses, car tyres, plastic bags and the smell of rotting food. This doesn't feel like pilgrimage territory to me. It's more like a rubbish tip on the edge of town. Our torches illuminate the orange eyes of the feral cats that have taken over the rubbish heap. We have made a wrong turn.

Cici blurts out, 'No way can I carry this pack all the way to Santiago! What were we thinking?'

The sun hasn't risen yet. With the weight of these packs, it will be a challenge to walk for most of the day, let alone a thousand kilometres. How did we not fully comprehend the physical challenge until now? We stand around in the darkness feeling the weight of our folly pressing down on us.

'Let's go back and start again tomorrow,' I say. 'We need to return to lighten our packs. We can offload some stuff, and then start out again tomorrow morning.'

I am secretly excited by the prospect of returning to our hotel, lazing in a cafe in one of the squares and enjoying another day in Seville. Who cares if we put it off for a day? If we start out again tomorrow, we'll only be a day behind.

A bluish morning light appears in the sky and turns to orange with the promise of a hot day ahead. We don't turn back. We continue walking in silence. An hour later, we have left the city behind and entered an industrial area. I pause to rest in the middle of the road when suddenly a rubbish truck hurtles around the corner without its lights on. I leap half way across the road as it disappears around the corner narrowly missing me. I breathe in its dust and the waft of rubbish. I look up at the growing light in the sky and laugh nervously.

Melbourne to Seville
Chapter 1

So, Remind Me Why We're Doing This

The pilgrim route is a very good thing, but it is narrow. For the road which leads us to life is narrow; on the other hand, the road which leads to death is broad and spacious.

– *Codex Calixtinu, (*the first official guide to
the Camino de Santiago – twelfth century)

Cici

In June 2015, I attended a silent spiritual retreat for a week on Victoria's Bellarine Peninsula. One morning I walked into the library and scanned the rows of books on the shelves. *Walking the Camino* by Tony Kevin became my constant companion during free time on the retreat. I found myself being drawn into the author's journey, into the adventure and into the challenge. By the end of the week, I was hooked and committed to walking the path, the Camino Vía de la Plata.

Weeks later, I attended an information session on the Camino. There were 18 people of varying ages in the group, mainly women. As we introduced ourselves, I realised that I was the only person in the room who planned to walk the Vía de la Plata. Everyone else was walking the Camino Francés, or the French Way. I was also the only person who said they were walking a spiritual pilgrimage which I found curious at the time. The other attendees were motivated by the challenge, or wanted to explore the region's culture and history, or improve their fitness. I was beginning to think I was in the wrong room. The two lecturers, both women, were very knowledgeable and had walked the Camino Francés three times, but they hadn't experienced the Vía de la Plata. However, they assured me the principles would be the same. I was starting to feel that this was going to be a journey with a distinct difference, a feeling that would return to me often in the year to come, and during the Camino.

I learned that there are several Caminos or pilgrimage routes in Spain. The Camino Francés, from east to west, is by far the most popular: nearly 57% of all pilgrims who completed the Camino de Santiago in 2018 took this route (186,199 people). Only 2.79% (9,127 people) chose the Vía de Plata, which runs south–north between Seville and Astorga. The reason this route interested me was that at the time I was working with St John of God Rehabilitation Hospital in Melbourne as a pastoral carer. Tony Kevin began his pilgrimage from Granada. This was also where St John of God began his work with the poor and ill in the sixteenth century. My plan therefore was to begin my pilgrimage in Granada, walking the Camino Mozárabe, which links up with the Vía de la Plata, the route walked by Tony Kevin.

What is it that makes a person volunteer to endure such an arduous journey on foot in modern times? The ease of transport and information provides the opportunity to venture to places that were once unknown to most and to explore them like never before. Perhaps, too, the Camino's popularity is due to the need for humans to feel challenged, to find a greater sense of meaning and purpose in life when spirituality may no longer be a part of it. Some may feel that walking the Camino offers an answer to an absence of meaningful rituals or rites of passage.

I started reading the stories of other pilgrims' experiences and what led them to walk a Camino. I felt a strong need to gain some understanding of their journeys and what many thousands of people experience each year on the trail. I kept imagining what it would be like for me. It opened up questions. What am I made of? What am I prepared to endure? Where is my breaking point? Why am I prepared to push myself so far out of my comfort zone? I was on a journey of self-inquiry and a pilgrimage suddenly made perfect sense.

My husband, Mike, and I announced our pilgrimage at a family lunch. My adult sons were used to me doing things out of left field, and they were always supportive and not particularly surprised by the next idea, challenge or adventure that sprang to mind. They probably suffered through all the times I dragged them to my racquetball and volleyball games when they were small (fair enough – I went to all of theirs). I was a long-distance runner for years and would bring home a ribbon from yet another run and tell them about the next challenge – a half marathon, a marathon, opening this business and that business, bringing more dogs home, finding new homes for those dogs, founding a charity for people living with cancer, introducing them to their step-father for the first time, studying in New York, and so on and so on. I stopped running in my late fifties. I was tired of putting pressure on myself to meet the next goal and the next, and my lower back was telling me it was time to stop. Now, having reached my mid-sixties, I planned to take on this new challenge for a very different reason.

The planning and training began, and 15 months later, in September 2016, Mike and I flew to Granada. By this time, we had realised we were not fit enough to take the longer route from Granada across to Mérida to join the Vía de la Plata, which was disappointing for me. Also, our time was limited, so instead we explored the history, places of ministry work and haunts of St John of God over a few days before boarding a train to Seville to begin the pilgrimage.

Mike

El Camino means 'the Way'. A way. For me, it means 'away from the familiar'. Away from the familiar challenges, the familiar work, the familiar anxieties, the familiar boredom and disappointments, the familiar wins and successes, and the familiar periods of waiting for something exciting to happen.

As enticing as the Camino sounds, I'm unsure how I will handle being away from the familiar. I don't know whether deep down I really want an adventure. The familiar is predictable. It's comforting. It's like an old car you have grown to love. You know how it drives. I feel I've long traded excitement and the thrill of adrenaline for a ride that is comfortable and predictable.

In the month before leaving home, I have no time to reflect more on how I feel. Life is busy. I am organising work and putting things in place so that while we are away bills get paid and car repayments are automated, along with insurances, direct debits and tax payments.

I also need to find the time to sit down with my bookkeeper, Dina, who manages the budget. Eventually we meet near her office in Prahran. We are enjoying the sun as we sit in the outdoor area of a café near the corner of Chapel St and High St. She is a stylishly dressed lady who is planning her next holiday in Switzerland and a cruise on the Mediterranean. I explain I will be away for the next four months, beginning at the start of September. She looks at me with her latte in hand, squints, and says, 'The Camino? Isn't that a walk? You're taking four months off to go for a walk!'

Actually, we've set aside two months for our Camino, not four. I explain to Dina that the Camino Vía de la Plata is an ancient pilgrimage route through Spain. It means the 'Silver Way' and may be so-named because the Romans built roads along this route to access the silver mines near Galicia. The distance from Seville to Santiago is around 1,000 kilometres. That's like walking from our bayside home in Melbourne to Mildura, which is located in the top left corner of Victoria, and then walking all the way back. Or like walking to Canberra and then adding a couple of hundred kilometres more.

When I explain the pilgrimage to friends and (some) clients, I usually begin by saying something like, 'So we are planning on *walking* the Via de la Plata.' They respond with a pause and then say, 'So are you walking it?' I understand that people have trouble absorbing the concept as most people expect that if you travel to Spain, it's for a holiday – perhaps shopping, sight-seeing in Barcelona and drinking good cheap wine on the Costa del Sol. When you tell someone you're going to walk with backpacks for about a thousand kilometres, it makes sense that they struggle to comprehend it. I wonder why I haven't struggled more to comprehend it too. But no, I have decided that the Camino is the way to go and that a pilgrimage is preferable to a 'mere' holiday. The next question people usually ask is 'why?' It is a question I welcome because I haven't really given it enough thought. Each time I reply, I am trying out a new answer to see how it feels. The truth is: it was my wife's idea.

Dina fixes her eyes on me.

'So you're walking this? Seriously? Why would you do that when you can drive across Spain in one of those zippy little things. Y'know…a convertible with a boot full of champagne. You're going to walk it?'

I tell Dina that it's the tradition to walk it, that's just the way you do the Camino. You're not meant to be a tourist who races through the towns leaving a trail of empty champagne bottles. It's all about slowing down and appreciating the journey.

She turns her gaze on me again. (I have always appreciated her directness).

'Why are you doing this Mike?'

I return her gaze and then look away. I take a sip of coffee and reply, 'I'll tell you when I get back.'

This is not the first time that I am confronted with my lack of a compelling reason for taking four months off and spending two months of those walking with a backpack. At a family gathering in August 2016, shortly before we left, I listened to Cici tell the story of how our plan came about and her moment of epiphany when a library book caught her eye.

Since giving up running, Cici had been searching for a new challenge. Three years before, she had graduated from the One Spirit Seminary in New York and been ordained as an interfaith minister. The Camino was a natural fit for her need for a physical challenge, and it had a spiritual angle as well. The spirituality part was, frankly, a slippery concept for me. All I knew was that I liked walking.

The idea of having the time to walk through what I imagined would be picturesque Spanish countryside appealed to some romantic notion of fleeing my life at this time. I imagined hiking enthusiastically along verdant Spanish pathways and across mountain passes to small villages where my arrival was rewarded with delicious tapas as I pushed back the boundaries of my hitherto unadventurous spirit. Why be a tourist when I could be on an adventure? And the thought of being by my wife's side as we walked down a dusty road awash with the soft colours of a sunset sounded wonderful. At the family gathering my brother-in-law brought me back to reality with a question: 'And what about your reason, Mike?'

All eyes turned to me, and I said unhesitatingly, 'I'm with her.'

Fast-forward to September 2016, and we are in Oxford, England, visiting old friends, Francis and Akemi, on our way to Spain. Cici had corresponded with Francis for 35 years since her early days working at the Bourne & Hollingsworth department store in London. They had become our UK family with whom we looked forward to spending time with on this trip.

The weather is warm and I feel my body unwind as the pace of life slows down. I have decided to start a journal. This morning I try to come to grips with my own reasons, spiritual or otherwise, for doing this walk, apart from wanting to support my wife and take time off from work.

I write, 'So why am I doing this Camino?' [Long pause]

'I like to walk.'

After about ten minutes of reflecting on this, I close the journal.

I've always found trekking to be calming. Cici and I enjoy walking in the Victorian Alps around Dinner Plain, Mt Hotham and Mt Feathertop. In 2006, I participated as a team member in the 100 kilometres Oxfam challenge over two days, and more recently I walked part of the Great Ocean Walk, which follows the coastline of southwest Victoria.

Each time I've completed a long hike I've felt a sense of near euphoria. I've felt I have accomplished something. Trekking seems to fulfil a primal need I have to be advancing, to be moving forward. I can walk at a pace that is unhurried and with no particular goal other than to arrive at the end of the day in a new town where I can hang up my walking poles and kick off my boots. The exciting uncertainty of what will happen in between is liberating. The thought of it makes me smile.

In my office there is a framed postcard of a dog running free after someone has forgotten to close the gate. The caption reads, 'Party like someone left the gate open'. The dog is a Jack Russell, and his tongue is lolling out as he runs across a field. He looks so happy and free. The past few years of work have not felt particularly free. I have often felt the pressure of running my business, including some months where there is too much work on and there is the suffocating feeling of 'not enough'. There are periods when I wake up feeling I haven't slept enough, and then my next thought is that I don't have enough time in the day to get through all the things that need to be done. At the end of the day I feel relieved – I got through it – yet there is still the nagging thought that I didn't get enough done.

The thought of leaving all that behind and walking without this familiar burden, slows my breathing. Walking for days on end will mean, I hope, that I can leave behind all the thoughts, worries and planning that are my daily companions. If I could walk for two whole months and in that time glance at my watch only casually, and not because I am rushing to get to my next meeting, or racing against the minute hand to click 'send' and email a report that a client has been expecting. The luxury of taking two months off, just to walk! Yes, that's a good reason to do the Camino.

While in Oxford, I find a book at a local bookshop, *The Hidden Pleasures of Life*, by Theodore Zeldin. Sitting in a pub, I reflect on the following passage:

I do not wish to spend my time on earth as a bewildered tourist surrounded by strangers, on holiday from nothingness, in the dark as to when the holiday will end, stuck in a queue waiting for another dollop of ice-cream happiness. I am conscious that I have tasted too few foods, experienced too few forms of work, nibbled too hesitantly at the mountains of knowledge surrounding me, loved too few people, understand too few nations and places. I have only partly lived and my only qualifications for writing this book is that I would like to know more clearly what a full life could be.

I read this a second time and think, *Memo to myself: I need to have more experiences in my life.*

The pub where I'm reading is on the banks of the River Thames near Folly Bridge, a short walk from the main part of Oxford and the famous university campus. Sitting outside in the shade of the awnings, I feel the march of time slow down and the firm pressure I have always applied to the accelerator of life ease off a bit. The air is unusually warm and fragrant with summer smells, and filled with the sounds of people enjoying each other's company.

The afternoon sunlight has a softness about it that sends my mind and my body to a sweet place of reverie. Maybe the English beer has gone to my head, but I feel the awakening of an appetite for something more from life as I re-read the Zeldin quote. As my friend Stuart, an erstwhile walking companion, used to say when staring at some challenging-looking terrain on the path ahead, 'Bring it on!'

That evening, heading back to our bed-and-breakfast on the outskirts of the old town, we pause on Folly Bridge to snap a photo of an unusual phenomenon in the sky. The setting sun seems to have a long trail of smoke, giving the illusion that it is falling out of the sky and plummeting to earth. It looks as if it is falling somewhere close by behind the spires and rows of gabled roofs. I'm not usually a superstitious person, so I surprise myself when I hear myself say out aloud, 'I hope this is not a bad omen!'

We have arranged to spend five days in Granada with American friends before travelling to Seville to start our trek. The first night we stay in a small hostel on one of the main boulevards, the Gran Via de Colon. The morning after we arrive in Granada, my first thought when I look out the window of our room across the rooftops towards the mountains in the distance is, 'Why have I never been to this city before?'

Already I love Granada's large boulevards and grand buildings. I love the huge ornate porticos where you push open a heavy door to find yourself in the cool of a marbled foyer facing a beautiful staircase or an antique lift, the kind with metal cage doors that you have to roll back. And I love the mix of ancient, Moorish and classical architecture. This is the old Jewish quarter and this is the Latin Quarter. This is where the artists lived and loved, and this is where the Catholics and the fascists built their monuments to power, and goose-stepped around the square. It is like no other city I have visited, and my slumbering desire for new experiences and the unfamiliar is awakened once more. I'm reminded of the excitement I felt when I first visited New York. These are cities that say, 'Look!'

I wander up to the rooftop with a coffee. It's nine o'clock in the morning and the heat is beating down. I feel the tiredness in my body as my mind begins to let go of thoughts of work and clients. Any momentary guilt evaporates as I think that there is nothing I have to do this week. There on the hill above the city is El Alhambra, a fortress-like structure with the remains of a garden built by the Moors. It was their attempt to re-create heaven on Earth. They built this amazing garden in a region of baking-hot, dry summers by creating an irrigation system to water the plants and trees. It makes me think of Arthur, my elderly neighbour back home, whom I am trusting to water my tomato plants and fruit trees, and I begin to worry that he has already forgotten about my garden. My worry quickly passes, however, and I enjoy spending the rest of the day meandering through the lanes, squares and pathways of this city.

Historically, Granada was one of the last strongholds of Muslim civilisation in Spain. Christians, Jews and Moors lived here in harmony for many, many years. It is important for us, but for Cici especially, to see the historic places where St John of God carried out his ministry. We pass through the gate of the hospital where he cared for people with mental illness (a revolutionary idea for its time) instead of letting them be thrown into prison. In the courtyard, we admire the stonework and frescoes on the walls that had faded with time. The modern 1980s brick version of the St John of God hospital is right next door.

We spend the rest of the day walking through the maze of lanes. Later, we come across a small square where a guitarist plays masterfully. I don't play the guitar but I can appreciate the skill and passion he puts into his performance. This is how God would play the guitar. I stand watching, and then I see something that escaped me because I was so transfixed by the music: he is blind.

That night in the main square, Plaza Major, we watch flamenco dancers performing for tourists. I once saw a performance in Melbourne that put me to sleep, but tonight the experience is electric. The dancers are passionate and full of fun and laughter; their enthusiasm is infectious. The sounds of feet stamping and hands clapping echoed against the buildings on the perimeter of the square. Is it possible? – I can feel my feet wanting to move! We enjoy the sight of small children, who are so engaged and uninhibited that they twirl and stamp their feet – they just can't help but join in.

After our first night in Granada, we move into an Airbnb up on the hill. From the rooftop, where there are chairs and a dining table, we have views across the city to the mountains, the Sierra Nevada ranges, in the distance. As the sun sets the four of us sit down to a wonderful dinner of tapas prepared by our friends, Els and Andy. We raise our glasses to the adventures ahead: 'Here's to the unknown!'

For our last night in the city, Els booked a table at a restaurant. I need to finish an email first (I'm still letting go of the need to check in with work back home), so the others go ahead of me. 'I'll catch up soon,' I say. I have Google Maps. What could possibly go wrong?

This day is part of the month-long festival celebrating the Patroness of Granada, the Virgen de Las Angustias. Leaving the house, I wind my way down to the Plaza Major. Thousands of people have come out to line the streets as the religious procession gets into full swing. 'Procession' is an understatement: this is a mass movement of Spanish Catholics along the main boulevard of Granada, a great long river of people in costumes and regalia singing and carrying candles and large religious icons. It is a sombre version of the colourful annual Moomba parade in Melbourne.

The river seems to stretch to the horizon and it is impossible for me to cross the road. When I realise I am now 30 minutes late and there is no natural break or pause in the procession, I decide to make a run for it. I climb over the barrier and temporarily become part of the procession, walking alongside the devout participants, but conspicuously without candle and religious garb. I am caught in the current of this human river and being carried away from where I should be heading. Then an opportunity comes and I break off and climb over the barrier to get to the other side of the street. The other side is no different; it's packed with people, making it impossible to move about easily. For some reason, I can't get a signal on my phone. Being lost in a foreign city and having no means of communicating with your wife, who has not brought her phone, and who is no doubt this minute waiting and becoming concerned, adds a certain something to the experience of being late. I start to feel panic rise in my throat. I don't know whether I'm concerned about not knowing where I am, or that Cici will be worried as well. It's probably both.

When I was six, I was separated from my mother in Woolworths one Friday afternoon. I hung around the socks on the ground floor until a kindly stranger bent down, looked at me closely, and said, 'Are you lost, little boy?' Then he hoisted me up in the air from under my armpits so I could see over the heads of the people in the store and identify the short, dark-haired figure of my mother. I remember the terror of being so small and the relief of being lifted up. But now there is no one to lift me up and Google Maps is kaput.

I have a brain wave: I can ask for directions in Spanish! At least I know the name of the restaurant and the street it's on. I can put to use all those weeks of practising Duolingo. The challenge, however, is not asking the question or making myself understood, but understanding the response when it is delivered rapidly by someone who is more interested in watching the procession behind me. With help from some hand signals and pointing – down this lane, take a right turn at the end – I head off through the crowds, taking note of landmarks so I can retrace my steps if I need to. There's a jewellery store on a corner. There's Desigual, the store Cici keeps talking about, on another corner.

It is now an hour since I set out and I still have no reception on my phone and no means of sending a text to our friends. The noise of the procession and the crowds pushing against me feels overwhelming. I have always felt claustrophobic and unsafe in crowds, which is why I gladly stay away from sporting events in large stadiums. I ask three people for directions, but their explanations are confusing and disorientating. I am starting to unravel. I feel six years old again. Just breathe! I take a moment to calm myself and then walk more slowly down the lane of restaurants and shops. Oh no, I've been here before. I must be going around in circles. Then I see her. Cici is waiting for me outside a restaurant that I walked past 15 minutes earlier. I try to look calm and collected, but we embrace and I mumble into her hair, 'I was so worried. I had no way of contacting you.'

'Yes, I know. Me too.'

We are both surprisingly emotional and I think anyone watching us would have thought we had been reunited after years of being apart. I didn't know it then, but this was to be the first of many raw emotions I would soon feel. At times, I felt ashamed and I wondered if I was regressing. I had turned 50 earlier in the year. Aren't you supposed to have it together by then? I would later realise these feelings had always been a part of me, but I had become pretty good at keeping them down and out of sight. For the past 20 years, I had lived within a certain emotional range. This pilgrimage was already starting to test the limits of that narrow range – and we hadn't even started yet.

Cici

My relationship with Els and Andy, our American friends who had flown to Granada from the USA to spend some time with us before our Camino, was no ordinary friendship. It had been forged in times of grief, and we had journeyed together in a very special way. We met through mutual friends – my work colleague Tony, and his wife Giselle.

Tony was a keen runner who had run the Boston and New York marathons, and I was very much into fitness. After my divorce from my first husband, I decided I needed a challenge, and inspired by Tony, I began to train to run my first marathon in New York. This began my long-standing relationship with the city, which I travelled to three times for the marathon. One year I represented Australia in the International Friendship Run held the day before the big event. I ran with the Australian flag, which was a great honour and privilege.

In 2001, Tony, in his early fifties, was diagnosed with pancreatic cancer. His world fell in and so did Giselle's. I was working as an oncology massage therapist in Melbourne hospitals, and I treated Tony in his home quite a few times until his death in 2002. One of the people who cared for Giselle and comforted her in her grief was her American friend Els, who flew from the US to Melbourne to be with her friend. That's when I first met Els. Giselle, also in her fifties, was herself diagnosed with a tumour in 2008. Again, Els flew from the US to Australia to support and care for her friend, staying with her for six months until Giselle entered a hospice. I saw them as often as was possible and supported them in whatever way I could. By the time of Giselle's death in 2009, Els and I had formed a strong bond.

In the meantime, I'd met and married Mike in NYC in 1999 (the marathon co-ordinator, Di Tolley, and her daughter Lisa were our witnesses). I'd also begun studying to become a pastoral carer, and I'd established a charitable foundation to provide financial support for people living with cancer when they were too ill to work. I still enjoyed my work as an oncology massage therapist, but I was aware of a deepening sense of spirituality and a desire to work in a more connected way with people.

On one of the three further occasions I travelled to New York for my interfaith/interspiritual seminary studies, Mike and I trained it down to Fredericksburg, Virginia, to stay with Els and Andy in their home. When I graduated in 2013, they travelled up to New York for the ceremony and joined us in a celebratory meal along with some of our friends and family and other interfaith ministers.

When I told Andy and Els of our upcoming adventure in Spain, we hadn't seen them for three years, and they embraced the opportunity to spend a week with us in Granada before we headed off on our Camino.

Mike

Tomorrow we will begin our Camino, but today we walk around Seville admiring its ornate buildings and charming cobbled laneways, and enjoy visiting its cafés and restaurants. Everyone appears to be enjoying tapas and *cervezas* (beers) at the outdoor tables in the humid warmth of late September. We scan the streets looking for other *peregrinos* with walking poles and scallop shells swinging from their backpacks.

We visit the cathedral to collect our first pilgrim's passport stamp. The passport is recognition of our official status as *peregrinos*. Pilgrims are required to have it stamped at the various villages en route, and when they arrive at Santiago de Compostela, they will present their passports with its stamps to the relevant authorities as proof of having walked the Camino. On entering the dark, cavernous space of the cathedral, we are led to the church offices by a security guard, who holds up his hand to instruct us to wait while our passports are taken from us for stamping. Eventually, a laconic church official returns them to us; he seems distracted and says nothing, not even 'Buen Camino' (Have a good walk). It feels like a bureaucratic and unspiritual start to our pilgrimage.

Even though the cathedral is the formal start of the Camino, we decide not to start from there but further away from the centre of the city where there is a mural display of the Camino and a pathway leading out of the city of Seville – it is only a couple of kilometres away, but it feels more like an 'official' start to us. We set out to find this start so we will know where to go early tomorrow morning. It is over the bridge in a working-class part of town, and we find ourselves in an area with lots of outdoor cafés, white plastic chairs and tables, and large umbrellas with Coca Cola signs. We also find the local church where Cici feels inspired to ask for a private meeting with the priest, and to ask for a blessing. We are ushered into the padre's office, where he sees our Australian passports and his eyes widen in surprise. 'Ahh! AahOOstralia!'

We paused on Folly bridge in Oxford to watch this unusual sight in the sky – Mike wondered if it was an omen.

It's now official. Cici has her first sello (stamp) in her Credential del (Pilgrim Passport) from the cathedral in Seville.

'I need to have more experiences in my life': this revelation came to Mike one afternoon at The Head of the River, a pub in Oxford.

The Hospitaller Order of St John of God was born in the Spanish city of Granada. Its name is the Spanish word for 'pomegranate' and the city uses the fruit as its symbol.

Hermanos haceos bien a vosotros mismos dando a los pobres. San Juan de Dios (Brothers do good to yourselves by giving to the poor. Saint John of God).

St John of God (1495–1550) tended to the sick and poor at the Granada hospital that bears his name. It was important to Cici to visit this historic site.

Church in Seville where Cici and Mike received the *Bendición del Peregrino* (Pilgrims' blessing).

Our friend Els on the rooftop patio of our Airbnb in Granada.

Granada reawakened Mike's desire for new experiences and the unfamiliar.

One of the many plazas in Granada.

The gardens in the palace/fortress Alhambra sit atop the city of Granada and were intended to be a vision of heaven on earth.

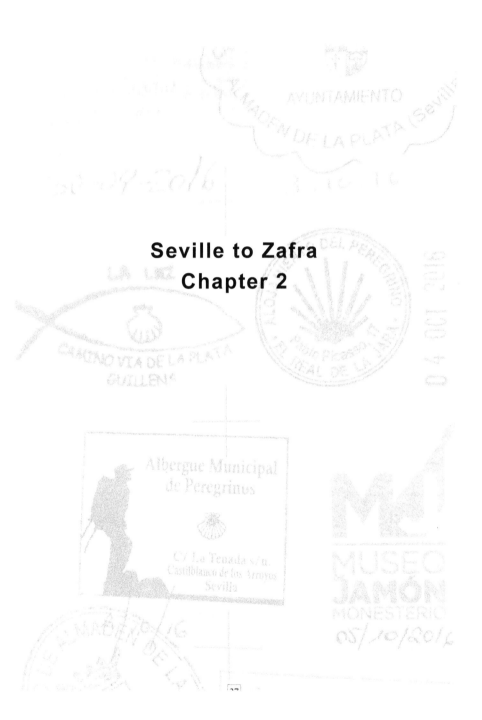

Seville to Zafra
Chapter 2

Bring It On

Mike

The start of our Camino wasn't marked by a grand archway or a formal entrance[1] with a sign that said, 'Welcome to the start of the Camino!' It started in a car park. In a respectful nod to the great tradition of this trek, there is a mural on a brick wall depicting a fifteenth-century pilgrim wearing a robe and carrying a walking staff and a gourd, an early version of a drink bottle. A sign provides a brief description of the history of the Camino. It will be a while before the sun peeps over the horizon, and in the darkness my eyes take in more details. The car park looks like a popular hangout for kids, skateboarders, graffiti artists and lesser 'artists' who just want to leave their tags on park benches and the mural wall.

For the next 1,006 kilometres, our route will be marked by yellow arrows, about the size of a man's shoe, painted on the sides of buildings, on signs, occasionally on rocks or gates, and even on tree trunks. The image of the scallop shell features in many of the signs.[2] In theory, all you need to do is follow the yellow arrows. Even where the arrows have disappeared or are worn out or rolled down a hill out of sight (if painted on a rock), there are always locals you can ask to point you in the right direction.

Many people walk as part of a group, and you can, of course, do the Camino as part of an organised tour with a Spanish-speaking guide. This makes good sense in many ways because in rural Spain very few people speak English. We are committed, however, to walking the Camino our way. We have decided this

---

[1] The official start of the Camino Vía de la Plata is at the cathedral.

[2] Legend has it that the shell, from the sea nearby, was carried as an original accreditation for completing the pilgrimage hundreds of years ago. It is seen on the path wherever you see a yellow arrow marker pointing the way to Santiago. Now you can buy one online whether you've done it or not.

means pushing ourselves beyond our comfort zones. The idea of heading into the interior of Spain with my Duolingo Level Four Spanish appeals to my sense of, 'Let's see what happens! What's the worst that could happen? We could get lost!' With hindsight, I can expand on a lot of other worse case scenarios, of which getting lost is the most appealing.

Setting out, we are nervously curious to see how we will experience all of this time to ourselves and to our thoughts. As we walk, the sun's morning colours spread across the sky. After a couple of hours, the factories and cyclone fences disappear and we reach the beginning of farmland and fields of cotton trees.

Nearing our first town we discover fellow walkers! There are three *hombres* on the other side of the road as we arrive at the town of Santiponce. Like us, they wear hiking boots and have their walking poles and packs from which swing the familiar scallop shells. We wave to each other and smile. We greet them in English and they respond in Spanish. Meeting some *compadres* for the first time lifts our spirits. We arrive at a café and order *cafés con leche* (milky coffee). Our fellow trekkers sit at another table chatting away. They seem to know each another well. The coffees arrive. Our courage is restored and it is as if our moments of panic and self-doubt never occurred. We are on our way.

Cici

Our guidebook, *Vía de la Plata* by Alison Raju, mentioned the threat of hostile dogs and advised us to have walking poles at the ready. We heard dogs a short distance away, but it was still very early and dark, so they were chained up. The sun would not rise until about a quarter past eight. We came across a horse in a cotton field; he was very curious and followed us along the dirt road for a little way, perhaps in the hope of food, or wanting a friend. We needed to discourage him, but I don't think he knew the meaning of 'Stay, boy'. Animals would become a constant reassuring presence in the weeks to come.

By mid-morning the heat had set in, so when we sighted a shady clump of trees by a dry creek bed, we peeled off our socks and boots and elevated our feet onto a log to rest. We had promised ourselves we would look after our feet from the start. Trying to get going again with swollen feet wasn't easy. Our Spanish café companions soon overtook us. 'Hola!' they called out as they ploughed on by. I didn't feel so bad when I saw one of them toting a huge black umbrella. It dwarfed my little aqua number, which provided a little shade, but already I thought I might need to ditch it because I just couldn't keep holding it kilometre after kilometre. I threaded the end of the handle through my pack's chest strap for a while, but this was not the answer for the long haul. I've since found out it's possible to buy umbrellas specially designed to connect to a backpack.

We had hoped to reach the town of Guillena by lunchtime but the temperature slowed us up considerably. I was feeling the effects of the overwhelming heat, an overloaded pack, and aches in every part of my body. I had to think of something else to trick my brain and body into walking this last leg.

The day before, exploring Seville, we had come across a lovely church where there was a service in progress. We entered, sat in the back listening to the Spanish and marvelled at the classical architecture. I loved the feeling of connectedness between the church and its community. After the service, I wrote a note in Spanish for the assistant to give to the priest. He motioned for us to wait and disappeared into the back of the church. Several minutes passed before he returned, gesturing for us to follow him to the priest's rooms where we were welcomed. My note had said we were beginning our pilgrimage to Santiago de Compostela the next day and would he offer us the *bendicion del peregrino* (the pilgrim blessing) and stamp our *credenciales* (pilgrim's passports). We had already had our passports stamped in the cathedral the day before, but having them stamped in this small church, which felt more intimately connected to its community, had greater meaning for me.

My religious roots are Anglican, but this Catholic priest didn't ask any questions. With a kind smile, he asked us to stand in front of him as he placed his stole around his neck and found the page he needed in his book. He read, and laid his hand upon our heads in turn. Gentle and compassionate, he was fully present to us. He slowly closed the book, held it against his robe, and said a prayer, all in Spanish, of course. Then he took our hands in his and wished us 'Buen Camino'. I was overcome with emotion and gratitude; tears filled my eyes. It had been 15 months to the day since I had conceived the notion of this journey. A great deal had happened in our lives in that time, both professionally and personally, and now the journey was finally real. The priest's blessing felt like a confirmation of the commitment, discipline and faith I had needed to make it a reality. Along with the ritual that accompanied it, the blessing was very significant for me.

Today's heat, which was in contrast to the cool interior of that church, was starting to seriously take its toll on me. Arriving in Guillena, 23 kilometres from our starting point, I was too exhausted to walk any further, so Mike left me under a tree in a children's park while he went to find our first night's accommodation. He soon returned to carry my backpack the half a kilometre further to a private albergue.

Mike

On our first day of the Camino, we walked from 6 in the morning until three o'clock in the afternoon. I have real doubts that we will be able to walk to Santiago with this weight on our backs. Seriously, I would be happy to hang up my walking boots and take a train, a bus or a taxi to Santiago. But I know that for Cici, to not fulfil her goal of walking to Santiago as an authentic pilgrim (as she perceived it) would be unthinkable.

That evening we have our first experience of Camino accommodation. Albergues provide low-cost, no-frills dormitory-style bunk rooms for pilgrims. The facilities are basic, comprising a shared kitchen and shared bathrooms. Checking in, we are required to understand and confirm that we agree to follow the house rules, which the manager's 12-year-old daughter, who is learning English at school, translates. As I struggle to make sense of the times when the albergue is locked at night and when we need to check out in the morning, an English-speaking guest suddenly appears and steps in to help. He speaks much better Spanish than I do, and he manages to translate the questions I am trying to ask, as well as the manager's responses. He introduces himself as Dan; he's doing the Camino with his wife, Lea. Maybe we can have dinner together tonight?

After the dramas of the morning, I have no regrets that we didn't head back to Seville to regroup, go searching for a baby stroller for Cici's pack and spend the afternoon in one of the cafés. I am feeling energised that we have made it to our first milestone and have arrived at our first albergue. My adventurous spirit returns. I suggest that we explore the local area and check out some bars or cafés for some takeaway meals for tonight. We are disappointed that we can only find a local fast-food shop so we head off in search of the *supermercado* (supermarket) to stock up for dinner.

That evening, we eat dinner on the roof-top area of the albergue, overlooking an old bullfighting ring, and share our meal with our new friends. We have tinned Portuguese sardines, crusty bread, containers of tapas and *jamón*, goat cheese and a bottle of Spanish wine. We enjoy the food and the conversation at the end of a very challenging day. The sun throws its light and colours across the clouds and the flat dry landscape that is typical of Andalusia. Knowing there are others with whom we will share our journey assuages my fears of trudging a long and lonely trek. Dan and Lea, both retired, are from Saskatoon, Canada. They have already walked the Camino Francés, but this is their first time on the Vía de la Plata. They are both surprised we have chosen the Vía de la Plata as our first Camino.

'Well, most people do the Francés,' Lea says. 'The Vía de la Plata is longer. It's hard if you don't have Spanish.'

Dan grins. 'Yes, there are less people and that means more time with yourself. You have lots of time to explore every nook and cranny of your mind on the Camino.'

It doesn't sound promising. I begin to understand why medieval magistrates punished people by sending them on the Vía de la Plata. If spending all that time in contemplation of their sins didn't send their minds over the edge, the brigands and thieves would surely get them. Despite this grim portent of what lies ahead, I feel happy. If we can have moments like this at the end of our days in the company of fellow pilgrims with whom we can share a meal and talk about our experiences over a glass of red, then walking for hours under the scorching sun might just be worth it.

Cici

When we arrived at the Guillena albergue, we were greeted by welcoming hosts, a clean shower, and surprisingly, a room to ourselves with twin beds. After a shower, I bandaged my finger where I had cut it on the old wire soap holder in the shower, tended to a couple of blisters that were developing on my toes, and dabbed cream on a cold sore on my lip, which had blistered in the sun. Now all doctored up, we decided to explore.

It would be dark when we left the following morning, so we went in search of the way out of town. We passed a small plaza, a church, and interesting little homes in the smaller laneways. The village was old, with the modern creeping in – there was a supermarket and takeaway shop. We came across Lea and Dan in the main street as we were checking out a café-restaurant in search of dinner. They had bought food, and we asked them about their plans. In small towns in Spain, the restaurants (if there are any) rarely open before 8.30 or 9 pm, and eating at that hour was too late for us because we had to be up before sunrise the next morning. We had no choice but to visit the supermarket. We also needed supplies for the following day: water, bread rolls, a tin of sardines, a couple of pieces of fruit each (we chose mandarins instead of oranges because they weighed less) and some mixed lollies.

When we arrived back at the albergue, the Spanish pilgrims were singing away and cooking up a large pot of pasta in the communal kitchen. They asked us to join them for dinner. This gesture was wonderful but we had agreed to meet Lea and Dan, who had just headed up to the rooftop, so we declined and thanked them. We felt grateful to be included. I was starting to feel a connection to our fellow pilgrims and the evolving camaraderie I had read about; this was the beginning of my feelings of belonging with my new tribe.

With *vino tinto* (red wine) in hand, we climbed a narrow staircase. The rooftop was sparsely equipped with a concrete tub for washing, a rope clothesline where pilgrims hung their socks and T-shirts to dry, and a small plastic table and chairs. We joined Lea and Dan to share conversation and a meal together in the now cooler evening breeze, feeling a strong sense of gratitude for a tasty meal, a safe place to rest, and a toast to a new friendship.

As the sun began to set on our first day, and the sky blazed with splashes of gold and strawberry hues in all directions, I reflected on the day and what I was grateful for: the beautiful cool morning air, the gentle presence of the horse, an oasis of shade in which to remove our shoes and socks, making it into town, the kind gesture of the Spanish pilgrims, and of course meeting Lea and Dan. We were all silent, staring and drinking in this heavenly panorama with weary eyes and exhausted bodies. In the silence, I was able to hear my heart and soul whisper: Welcome to the Camino.

All was quiet as we woke the next morning at five o'clock. As it says in the story, not a creature was stirring, not even a mouse. Some exhausted *peregrinos* were snoring, but that's another story. We tried to be quiet as we dressed, tended to my feet, and packed our things. We wanted to head out by six to walk as far as we could while the morning air was still cool. I don't think the others liked having their slumbering stillness disturbed so early. We were yet to learn the unspoken rules on this Camino, which included lights out around 9 pm, and no packing up or making noise before 6 am. They're not written in stone, but it's important to observe them.

They say the body is able to anaesthetise itself when it is in pain. I responded to the hardship of the previous day by starting out without stopping to think how I was feeling physically, walking five kilometres in the dark with our head torches. We were driven by anxiety, anticipating the heat to come; we knew it lurked and would soon pounce and envelop us in a lather of sweat.

Today was only a 20-kilometre day, but it was very difficult, with a steep ascent, and then a descent into Castilblanco. Stomach-churning smells from pig farms wafted in the heat. Walking ahead of me, Mike would call out, 'Incoming!' I prepared for it by dousing my bandana in eucalyptus oil, wrapping it around my nose and mouth until the assault had abated. The absence of a breeze didn't help. Lea told me later that she didn't mind the smell at all; she loved the pigs.

We had both woken up with very sore shoulders from carrying our packs and we started to think about ditching everything that wasn't absolutely necessary, regardless of the cost of sending it home. But it was impossible to define 'necessary' so early in the walk. Under the circumstances, we were pleased with our time of five hours from Guillena to Castilblanco.

Our arrival routine was to become very familiar over the next two months: find a pilgrim refugio or albergue, choose a bunk, stash the packs and shower. Tonight was to be our first experience of a municipal albergue with an open-plan bunk area. I was one of only two women staying; all the other *peregrinos* were men, and the bunks were only an arm's length apart. I hadn't given any thought to this sort of situation, and I felt vulnerable. I know it sounds naïve and precious, but I really didn't know whether I could cope. I told Mike I couldn't stay. We left our gear and went in search of a hostel or pension, without success. Then I remembered having seen a 1970s-style hotel, a tad past its heyday, as we entered the town earlier.

We returned to pick up our packs, and Mike did his best to explain my predicament to the manager. I don't know why I left it to him to explain. Maybe it was because everything was feeling very male orientated, and trying to speak Spanish was even more difficult when I was hot and tired. It was embarrassing, and the manager looked confused about our sudden decision to leave. We slowly made our way up the hill to the hotel, where we ran into Lea and Dan. They were staying the night there as well, which made me feel a bit better about not staying at the albergue. They told us it was Dan's 60th birthday that day, and at some point, we would share a meal to celebrate.

Mike

We start out again in the dark as the glow of the morning sun spreads across the sky, walking along bitumen roads that eventually turn to deeply rutted tracks. I think of colder days to come when we won't have to rise so early to beat the heat. We arrive at a run-down café at an intersection. Large trucks are parked out front; their drivers, wearing high-vis vests, are inside staring in silence at the Spanish news on TV. I venture in to see what the breakfast fare is – it is the standard *tostadas* (toasted rolls with tomato purée, salt and olive oil) and coffee. The coffee is good – always good – but I will need to wait to return to Melbourne before I can enjoy poached eggs or a sweet pastry with my flat white.

We set off again, followed by the almost constant barking of angry-sounding dogs in the distance. For some reason, I spend a lot of the morning thinking about my parents, and I return to the question of why I am doing this walk. I settle on the thought that I'm doing it to honour my parents and their sense of adventure.

My dad grew up in Denmark, but as soon as he was old enough, he backpacked around Europe, especially southern Europe and as far as North Africa in the 1950s. I have an album of small sepia photos of his travels showing him and his older brother. One of the photos shows them in baggy white shorts and carrying rucksacks. They both look fit and tanned. There are even a few photos of them in Spain where the landscape is mountainous and completely unlike what I am experiencing. Wouldn't it be amazing if our walking paths crossed, though 50 years apart? I play with this thought for the next few kilometres. What if we were to meet in some time-space aberration? What would I say to him? And what would he say to me?

'Hi Dad, cool shorts! Can I walk with you a bit?'

'Do you know, in a few years, you will end up living at the other end of the earth in a working-class suburb of Melbourne? You'll drive your bronze-coloured Ford Falcon every day to work in a factory. You will like the job because you are good with your hands and so skilled when it comes to fixing things. You will find the bosses difficult, but your workmates will love and admire you because you stick up for the underdog, the new workers, the new immigrants and anyone who struggles with English and fitting in.

One day, when you are a lot older, I will introduce you to my wife Cici. I will always remember the day – you will be in your blue dressing gown and slippers and you will be so happy to meet her because I will tell you we are getting married.

[I wouldn't tell him this, but he would meet Cici in a hospital – he would learn of his cancer diagnosis a few months before being due to retire from his job of 40 years, and he would soon die from it.]

So Dad, can we walk this next bit together? There is so much I never got to talk about with you…'

My mother grew up in Japan and left her homeland to become a young representative of a trading company in Australia. She opened an office in Pitt Street, Sydney in the early 1960s where she set about building an import-export business and employed a team of salesmen. She placed her desk at the front of the office on blocks of wood so it was higher than her employees. She placed their desks in a line all facing hers (one behind the other), rotating the top salesmen to the front of the line and moving them down the line if they didn't reach their monthly targets. With no experience in managing, especially not Australian men who were not used to answering to a diminutive Asian woman, she had her work cut out for her. She had a lot of grit then, but by the time I left home (long after she retired), she had few reserves of courage left and struggled to trust life. I think a big part of that was not feeling at home in Australia and living with the pain of her past. Growing up during the Second World War, my mother lost her father at a very young age, and I suspect she always blamed herself for this tragedy.[3] With their dad gone, she and her family lost their home and sources of income as a result of the re-organisation of Japan's economy. Looking at photos of her as a young woman, I see a glimpse of her character then; she has a determined steady gaze as she looks at the camera. That all changed, and in mid-life her fears came to rule her as she tried to control the unpredictable in her world, which included my life and for a while, my career. For the first time ever, I wondered what she must have went through when she came to live in Australia and what it must have felt like for her moving into her first home after she married Dad in the outer suburb of Dandenong.

---

[3] Her dad had not died in the war. One morning at breakfast my mother, who was very precocious for a ten-year-old, was reading the paper. She warned her dad not to take the short cut through the forest as there was a report of an escaped criminal at large. Unfortunately, he didn't heed her warning and was murdered by the escapee

In their marriage, my parents walked separately on their long lonely Caminos. Mum's life was transformed when Dad died at 67 of multiple myeloma and she no longer felt a duty to look after or care for anyone. I believe she had finally let go of her feelings of being responsible for her father's violent death. Now, she allowed herself to discover some of life's pleasures, like mangoes, which she tasted for the first time in her seventies. She was so delighted with this that she had to call me in the middle of the night to tell me. She discovered that dogs had personalities, 'just like people!', which was an epiphany for her. Her insight confirmed in her mind that there was a God after all (her words).

I thought a lot about my mother and father in the early parts of the walk. I was never very close to them when they were alive, and I regret that. It turns out Dan was right. As I struggled with the discomfort and heat during that first week, I spent a lot of time exploring memories and those nooks and crannies he spoke about which helped me avoid being present to what I was doing.

Cici

In training for the Camino, we had spent more than a year mapping out and tackling the many one-day walks. We'd also wanted to simulate the experience of walking all day, staying somewhere overnight, and walking again the next day, so we spent several weekends away from home. We aimed for consistency and discipline in our training.

During that year, however, the health of our dear friend Shirley had begun to deteriorate. Shirley had recently celebrated her 90th birthday, and she had been quite independent for as long as I had known her. But it was time for her to explore assisted-care options. My heart goes out to those who reach a stage in life when they realise that major change is now inevitable, but not welcome. Everyone experiences it differently; for some, it brings a fear of losing the person you have always been and surrendering to a life of dependence. This often leads to feelings of trepidation, disempowerment, vulnerability, and of course, a lack of independence. These were Shirley's fears. Supporting her and spending time with her during this process had taken time away from our training, which meant that we were not fit enough to begin our Camino in Granada and take the longer route. I wouldn't have had it any other way.

On day three, we rose before dawn as usual and began packing to set out from the hotel. Mike logged on to the iPad, intending to email our sons to tell them that all was well. But instead, he found an email saying Shirley had died.

She would never read the letter I had promised and already sent. We sobbed as we prepared for the day ahead, dressing my two blisters and padding my right collarbone against the pressure of my pack's shoulder strap. The news was difficult to accept, but it did not really come as a surprise. We would miss Shirley very much. After a light breakfast, we headed out to meet the day quietly and very much in reflective mode, remembering our friend.

Later that morning we zigzagged our way up a steep, red gravel hill. At the top, we met a group of Spanish pilgrims who sat to catch their breath and have a break. They told us that a few weeks before, with the heat around 50 degrees Celsius, a fellow pilgrim had had a heart attack and died at the top of that hill. We had also heard of a Japanese pilgrim walking the Camino Francés in the north who died in the snow of hypothermia. His walking companion was rescued. This had become a sad day in a few respects. When we reached Almadén de la Plata, we found a place to have our credentials stamped, and a nice clean albergue where we had the first floor to ourselves – bonus!

In the days that followed, we struggled with the incessant heat. We decided we would walk seven days at a time and then rest two nights in the same town, where we would book into a hostel or hotel to get some washing done and rejuvenate. I think Lea and Dan were fitter than us as they rested after ten days. Some days, on this isolated route the animals were the only living beings we made contact with until we reached our day's destination. We passed large herds of goats, lonely horses, cows wearing metal bells, and endearing donkeys with large expressive eyes and long furry ears. The cows were timid, just peeping over fences in curiosity, and we donated many an apple to the gentle-natured horses and donkeys.

By now, we had left Andalusia behind us and entered Extremadura. 'Madura' means harsh in Spanish, so you can guess what Extremadura means. Our guidebook noted that on this leg of the journey, a distance of 20 kilometres from El Real de la Jara to Monesterio, 'the sun will be your enemy'. Great! Sure enough, there was no protection from the sun except a little shade in the shadow of a stone wall where we sat to take a break. We had asked the manager of the café where we had our morning coffee to pack us a couple of rolls. I would soon learn to be more specific – we would get better at this. The rolls were dry, floury and filled with sliced fatty pork. I am a vegetarian, so a tiny tin of soya beans and an apple were my rations for the day.

Monesterio is famous for breeding black pigs, which are fed on acorns, and for producing *jamón*, (cured ham). As we walked into the town, we stopped at the first sign of civilisation and shade, which appeared to be a tourist information centre, where we had our credentials stamped. We noticed later that the stamp was from the *Jamón Museo* – (the Ham Museum)!

After a shower, we ate a late lunch at a café next to our hostel. We saw our new Canadian friends Dan and Lea walk into town, and they introduced us to a German pilgrim from Stuttgart, Anneliesl, who was a veteran Camino walker. So far it seemed we were the only novice pilgrims en route. Anneliesl had completed the Portuguese Way, the Camino Francés, and the Camino del Norte. She asked why we had chosen the Vía de la Plata as our first Camino. I explained the story around my work as a pastoral carer with St John of God and wanting to begin the Camino in Granada. Anneliesl told us what we were learning very fast: that the Vía de la Plata is the hardest, harshest, longest and most isolated of all the Caminos. We all had a good laugh at the irony of our choice and raised our glasses: 'Let's drink to that!'

When it comes to fitness, some Camino guidebooks state that you don't need to be very fit to walk the Vía de la Plata because you will get fit along the way. Maybe that's true for some people, but if you want to carry your own pack, walk without incurring injury and as a bonus, enjoy it, then being fit is a distinct advantage. The majority of this Camino traverses the Extremadura region, and while it isn't mountainous, the long, flat, rocky paths early on can play havoc with your feet and lower back. Many people start out with a pack that is so overweight that their physicality is pushed to its limits, and Mike and I were no exception: Mike's pack weighed 15 kilograms, mine 12. While arranging our pack, we had tried to cater for not only the heat but also the cold and the wet weather, which we expected further north, and perhaps there was a bit of a scarcity mentality at play too.

As novice Camino walkers we were working with the unknown and we feared leaving behind some vital piece of gear. I had heard of people posting gear home along the way, which I was certain wouldn't apply to us, but it did – several times. By the time we had walked two-thirds of the route, we were down to the bare essentials – eight kilograms for Mike and six for me. I was also feeling much lighter of heart, having not packed a mobile phone. I didn't use one for four months. What bliss! Mike took his mobile just in case we got into trouble of any kind (or our boys needed to call us in an emergency), but we used it only half a dozen times in 55 days.

After listening to Anneliesl, I reflected on the events that had led me to walk this route. If I had known at the start what she told us, I still wouldn't have been deterred by the harshness, the length or the isolation. The Vía de la Plata was the journey to which my heart and soul were committed. If someone told me that tomorrow I would need to run through a fire or swim through a flood, I would have said 'yes, okay', if this is what it takes to 'meet' myself. The thought of giving up never crossed my mind, and hearing from experienced pilgrims that we were doing the hardest of the pilgrim treks gave me a sense of pride. I don't know if pride belongs on a spiritual pilgrimage, but there you have it.

Mike

We found a room at the Hostal El Pilar in Monesterio where I removed my boots and socks to air on the balcony. Cici and I sank into our mattresses and enjoyed the feeling of our comfortable beds. I allowed myself to experience this pleasure for 10 or 15 minutes, but then other thoughts pressed down on me. How could we do this whole journey in this dry, hot landscape? Soon there was a small committee of critics gate crashing my moment of peace. What were you thinking? Why didn't you leave it another year when you're fitter? Shouldn't you be back home with your business? The antidote for those oppressive thoughts and questions was food. Fortunately, there was a café across the small square from our hotel – Manuel's café. Discovering that Cici was also hungry, I pull on my smelly boots and we walked downstairs into the bright glare of the sun. With a limited choice of *bocadillos* (sandwiches) or *sopa* (soup), we ordered bean soup and bread rolls – I was proud that I could now order lunch in Spanish.

(Manuel was typical of hospitable café owners on our trek and he later made us bocadillos with *jamón* and hard cheese, which he wrapped in aluminium foil for the next day). Like most of the restaurants and cafés we visited, this one was dark and brown inside. The tables, the chairs, even the fittings were different shades of brown, and the lights were turned off, possibly to conserve electricity.

In the gloom of the café, I thought of my childhood growing up in Dandenong in the early 1970s, and of visiting cafés with my dad when he went in search of a good coffee. Many of the cafés in Spain's interior reminded me of the 'coffee lounges' in the outer working-class suburb of Melbourne where I lived until I was ten years old: the same brown panelling, the same faded white-tiled floors, the same cigarette-vending machines.

Sitting outside, we enjoyed the soup and felt good even though our shoulders ached and our feet were sore. At the next table was a young German couple, Friedrich and Anna, who were doing a road trip in their Ford Festiva. Anna wanted to know how much time we were taking off from our 'regular' lives to travel.

'Four months!' said Friedrich, obviously shocked.

'Wow!' exclaimed Anna. 'But don't you run a business? How can you leave your business for that length of time?'

The hint of concern in her question was contagious, and I remembered having a similar conversation with our neighbours in Melbourne two months earlier. Heather and Kornel, a young couple, lived across the street from us and shared our interest in vegie gardens. I told them of our plans while looking at our harvest of carrots and tomatoes.

'Who takes four months off to go walking?' Heather said. She sounded astonished.

The question, and the implication that taking that sort of time off was lunacy, blindsided me. I don't remember what I said, but I walked home wondering whether I had thought things through. *Was I being irresponsible?*

From the start of the Camino we had walked past rows of abandoned shops and whole villages turned into ghost towns as the result of economic downturns. Anna's questions brought back my fear that while I dilly-dallied across Spain, my business was going to rack and ruin. Since my chat with Heather and Kornel, I had had time to think about how to justify walking away from my responsibilities. Now was my opportunity to deliver my rehearsed response, which went something like this:

'Well, Anna and Friederich, the real question should be why don't people think it is important enough to take time off to do this kind of thing? We cannot let our fears determine the course of our lives. Running a business is hard and challenging. Every business owner should take time off from their business. Four months is a long time, but the alternative can be burn-out.'

I explained that ten years earlier I had almost done that: I had almost burnt out from the stresses of running my consultancy. Cici and I had moved out of the suburbs and bought a house on the Mornington Peninsula close to vineyards and farms. It was a restorative time for me. I slowed down. I discovered gardening and developed new friendships, including with my 85-year-old neighbour, an Englishman with whom I enjoyed many afternoons playing chess in his garden and listening to stories of his life as a young civil engineer in Alaska.

Anna and Friederich nodded. Anna agreed with my little speech and said that her boss, who ran the architecture firm she worked for, was also on the brink of burn-out. He had developed a tic in recent years and would blink uncontrollably when she reported that a project had run over budget and behind schedule.

My speech might have sounded pretty good, but it hadn't convinced me I was doing the responsible thing. Was it going to be possible for me to take a break from 'me'? To become just Mike the *peregrino*, no longer Mike the consultant? Could I forget myself? Could I leave behind the baggage that goes with who I am? The worries, the hopes, my goals, my fears, and walk on like the man in the Johnny Walker whisky ad? Ahh, now that *would* be freeing.

Later that evening we caught up with Dan and Lea at a small restaurant. The tapas was exceptional and the wine wonderful as we sat outside in the laneway watching people returning to their homes at the end of the day. Most of them carried plastic shopping bags with groceries for the evening meal and I suspected not many would have the means to enjoy a meal in a restaurant mid-week. We were constantly reminded of how Spain was struggling to recover in the aftermath of the 2008–2014 economic crisis. How insulated we were in Australia from this economic earthquake that had laid waste to so many jobs, communities and families. I wondered what people thought of us: a couple of Australians doing this trek through their country. Did they see us as cashed-up tourists with nothing better to do? Did they resent us for it? We met some surly younger people serving in bars and cafés, but their manner seemed to convey their boredom and frustration with rural life and the lack of job opportunities rather than any kind of resentment. Youth unemployment hovered around 60% in this area. No, when I think about it, the sight of us both seemed to attract friendly greetings from locals, who would say '*Buen Camino*'. I went to sleep that night relieved that I could drift off easily without the committee of voices in my head questioning what I was doing. The company of our friends Dan and Lea was reassuring at many levels. I felt very much at ease with them. I was able to connect with other people who had chosen to leave their regular lives behind and accept that perhaps, I wasn't being irresponsible after all.

We have been walking for a week now and are still acclimatising to the dust, the heat and the flatness of the Meseta. We walk past fields of cotton and olive groves. I am constantly amazed at the absence of people – there are no farmers or workers in sight, only curious farm animals staring at two *peregrinos* walking in the heat of the day. It is the first time I have ever seen cotton growing, and on closer inspection I see how difficult it is to remove the cotton from the branches because of the thorns. It is amazing to think that these bushes produce the fibre that makes the clothes in the factories and sweat shops of distant countries. It starts here in the south of Spain under the harsh glare of the sun.

I have a favourite photo of Cici that captures our experiences of this first week. She has her back to the camera as she walks in the middle of the dusty road with featureless rocky fields spread out on either side of her. On the horizon, there is a small, lone figure (another *peregrino*?). Cici carries an umbrella to protect herself from the sun. We had imagined something different. We had imagined our days consisting of three to four hours of walking in the morning, then a rest of a couple of hours, and finally a stretch of two to three hours more walking before we arrived at the next town at the end of the day. But the lack of shade and the scarcity of towns in which to rest from the heat means we rarely have the chance to stop for a break in the middle of the day. Most days we push on through the heat in one long stretch.

Our packs are still too heavy. Most of the day we are too hot and tired to talk except in staccato bursts: 'Stop! Let's stop! Water…need to stop for water…' Or, when Cici's stuffed toy rabbit Pompy, our mascot, falls from one of the outer pockets of her backpack: 'Wait! Pompy! Where is he?' Looking back, we see Pompy sitting on the road, and we have to retrace our steps to retrieve him.

Today we have miscalculated the amount of time it will take us to cover the distance, and our race against the sun has an extra urgency to it. We spot some eucalyptus trees near a farm, remove our packs and sit in the shade. We pull off our shoes and peel off our socks to inspect our tender white feet. There is a cool breeze today for the first time, and while it is tempting to lie down to rest our heads on our packs and take a siesta, we cannot afford to waste time.

After 20 minutes, we continue walking and still there is no one to be seen. We have not seen anyone all day. Suddenly we come across evidence of farm workers: parked Toyota Hiluxes, old Renault vans and large farm equipment, including automated cotton pickers. Most of the cotton will be blown into large cages; loose fibres float and swirl in the air around us like down and feathers. There is a small grove of olive trees where we stop for a short break. Taking off the pack only to put it on again is too hard, so I leave mine on, and like Cici, I hang my walking poles on the olive branches to have a drink of water and enjoy the dappled shade of the trees before moving on. We cross the irrigation ditch and are back on the road.

Every break is welcome, but it becomes harder to pick up the rhythm of your stride afterwards. After a while, I turn around to look at Cici, who is behind me. I see she has forgotten her poles. She has left them at the olive trees, which are now about 500 metres behind us. The thought of walking back is unbearable; we must push on through the heat. If I had the energy, I would send out a volley of expletives, but I can only muster a sigh combined with one long, exasperated 'F@#%!'

I wait while she walks back to retrieve them, back past the farming equipment and the clouds of cotton. Squatting on the road, balancing myself with my poles, I watch until she is no longer visible. When she returns, I see that the energy has drained from her face. Her physical exhaustion shows in her slow, faltering steps. No words are spoken. Talking is too much effort.

We walk on to the distant town of Zafra, arriving on the outskirts close to mid-afternoon. The town lies across a river lined with eucalypts that are similar to the trees from home. Cici's pace has now slowed down a lot and she says she cannot go on much further. Soon we are over the bridge and I am relieved to see a large town promising cool bars, restaurants and air-conditioned accommodation. We have walked 28 kilometres today with temperatures in the mid-thirties.

There is a city park on the other side of the bridge and I help her off with the pack as she drops onto a bench in the shade. I leave her to rest while I head off in search of accommodation. It doesn't take long before I discover a jewel of a hotel in the heart of the town. Stepping into the lobby, I step through a portal into the privileged life of the former palatial home of a wealthy landowner of a bygone era. The enormous lobby, with its vaulted ceilings contains a large mahogany desk fronted by elegant chairs, and numerous antlers and boar heads on the walls reminds guests of the former owner's favourite pastime. A lady sits at the desk with her pen poised above a notebook as I stagger in with my backpack and poles. This is the place for us, I think, reaching for my credit card.

Cici

We had been on the trail for nearly a week, and the 28-kilometre stretch from Fuente de Cantos to Zafra was our longest yet. The vegetation was sparse, the landscape desolate. We passed through a town in the morning, but absolutely nothing was open. My blisters had become so painful around the 20-kilometre mark I could barely hold it together. There is a saying that the first seven to ten days of the Camino challenge you physically, the next seven to ten days challenge you psychologically, and from then on it challenges you spiritually.

When we arrived in Zafra, I sat in the park on a bench under the trees while Mike, again being very chivalrous, continued walking to find accommodation while I rested. He was exhausted too, but he didn't have any blisters yet. He came back excited for me to see the accommodation he had booked for us.

Our room was cool with very high ceilings. I looked into the full-length mirror attached to the front of the ornate brown wooden wardrobe. I took off my hat and removed the tie from my hair. I expected it to fall in oily clumps about my face but instead it remained matted to my scalp resembling a cleverly constructed nest any bird would have been proud to call home. I would need to find a hairdresser. I purposely hadn't packed shampoo and conditioner due to carrying yet more weight. I realise you can carry tiny tubes; however, with long hair it wouldn't have been adequate.

Later, after showering and washing our clothes, we stepped out into the narrow cobblestone street and weaved our way through the maze of laneways. This was our first experience of a medieval town dating from the thirteenth century and we were in awe. The laneways soon opened onto the Plaza Mayor, which was framed by stone cloisters and regal archways throwing their afternoon shadows across the square. We came across the familiar faces of some of the fellow *peregrinos* we had befriended in the past week. Life felt lighter again. The group included a couple, Marga and Jesús who lived in Santiago de Compostela. This was difficult for me to comprehend at first. From the moment I'd decided to undertake this journey, Santiago de Compostela had been, in my mind, a holy city akin to Jerusalem or Mecca, a shining beacon of spirituality. It was a place where, for centuries, pilgrims had arrived after walking hundreds of arduous miles, often in extremely poor states of health, and often having been assaulted and robbed along the way, to finally kneel and kiss the stone at the base of the statue of St James in the famous cathedral. Even today, for Mike and me, this pilgrimage was enormously challenging, taking us totally out of our comfort zone on many levels. But we had just come face to face with people who actually lived in Santiago! Surely nothing as ordinary as plain old urban living could exist in such a place. Yet Marga and Jesús lived a normal life there like thousands of others – meeting with friends, doing their grocery shopping, working out at the gym, just like we did in Melbourne.

Later, I asked Mike whether the fact that Marga and Jesús lived in Santiago had had an impact on him. 'No, not at all,' was the short answer. Meeting Marga and Jesús broke the spell under which I was walking. A good old dose of reality goes a long way towards removing the blinkers. Yet nothing about this Camino felt ordinary for me. Yes, there were many days that felt like drudgery, but the ordinary and the extraordinary can, and do, co-exist.

We had come to realise there are many different ways to do the Camino. Marga, for example, doesn't like to walk, but she has found a way to accompany Jesús in his passion for walking the Camino. They walk from one town to the next in a day the same way we do, but carry only a daypack between them. At the end of each day, Jesús hitches a ride back to the town where they started that morning and drives their mobile home to the new town. This way, they have all the comforts of home each night. Amazing! Some people pay to have their packs transported ahead to the next town and walk with a daypack. They have their accommodation booked for them in advance, and their meals prepared. Others stay in hotels and *paradores* (old palaces restored to luxury accommodation).

We caught up with our fellow pilgrims that evening and it was just what the doctor ordered. Our Spanish *compadres* were talking about us and grinning, and Marga translated: they found it amusing that we walked with long sleeves and long shorts or full-length trousers in the hot sun. We explained that we were used to it because of the high incidence of skin cancer in Australia. For them, it wasn't a concern.

We had now walked for seven days, but we felt so relaxed and energised by catching up with other *peregrinos* that part of us wanted to keep walking the next day. Then we thought of how wrecked we had felt coming into town and what we had put our bodies through this week, having covered 149 kilometres. It would be best for us in the long term to stay another day and rest up. We were gradually developing a new awareness of our bodies, and learning to balance our energy and our need to rest.

The next day, I found a hairdresser to have my hair washed. On my own, and out of my depth language-wise, I entered and spoke to a hairdresser who called a second who called a third who all spoke over each other at high volume and at such speed that it sounded like they were calling a horse race. I sat in a chair staring up at them as each offered encouraging looks and spoke to me with such confidence, inferring they knew what I wanted. Then, still in chatter mode, each in turn began touching my hair at varying lengths with their fingers imitating scissors.

There was a lot of interjections from me trying to get a word in edgeways in an attempt to answer, '*Si, si*', nod, nod, and then, shake of the head until I interrupted, '*sin corte de pelo por favor*' (no haircut please). Put under this pressure, my few CD Spanish classes were finally kicking in. We were past the point of confusion as I tried to explain that I didn't want my hair coloured or cut. Adding to the kerfuffle, I learnt that conditioner is not part of a hair wash but an extra treatment, which I needed having long hair. I felt embarrassed that they may have thought my hair always looked this disgusting. The excitement was over and they finally broke ranks losing interest when they realised I just wanted my hair washed and conditioned. I thoroughly enjoyed having a week's worth of dust and sweat rinsed away.

We emailed home for news of Shirley's funeral.

Bridge over the Rio Guadalquivir on the way to the start of the
Vía de la Plata in Seville.

The dust, the heat and the flat terrain were tough going – still only day two.

Stepping into our hotel in Zafra was like stepping through a portal into the privileged life of the nineteenth-century owner, Don Agustín Mendoza y Montero.

Checking our guidebook, Vía de la Plata by Alison Raju, as we arrive in Santiponce.

Happy-hour in Zafra with fellow pilgrims (left to right):
Dan, Jesus, Breza, Marga, Cici and Lea.

Considering the heat and steep climbs, we were pleased with our time of five hours
from Guillena to Castilblanco on day two.

Curious friends along the way.

Walking across the plains of Extremadura.

Marga and Jesús, from Santiago, whom we met on the trail.

Cici left her boots on a park bench in Zafra for someone else to use. Shoes were better suited to the conditions.

Mike with Domingo, the Monasterio café owner who provided us with soup and sandwiches.

The first of many signs to guide us. These would soon become familiar.

Monesterio, arguably the home of (ham) Iberico in Extremadura Spain.

In the first weeks, we saw few people but many animals including this Portuguese sheep dog guarding his flock.

Our first break after a long hot morning and Mike struggles to smile for the camera despite Cici's pleading.

Zafra to Cáceres
Chapter 3

TORREMEJIA

ALBERGUE TURÍSTICO

$10 - 10 - 16$

Archidiócesis de Mérida · Badajoz

Parroquia Sta. Maria la Mayor Mérida

$12 - 2016$

VILLAFRANCA
DE LOS BARROS

Albergue "EL CARMEN"

$9 - 10 - 16$

ALCUÉSCAR

$13 · 10 · 16$

DESARROLLO Y TURISMO SOSTENIBI

Hector Comes Along
for the Ride

Cici

Saying goodbye to Zafra, I stopped to leave my boots on a park bench for someone who could use them. Even though they still had more kilometres in them, they hadn't worked for me in the heat, whereas my spare shoes felt lighter and less cumbersome.

We began the day without a good night's sleep because our bedroom window had faced a narrow street adjoining a plaza that was noisy with pedestrian traffic until the early hours of the morning. It was our ninth day of walking. We had trouble finding our way out of the city, and the delay meant that we suffered more time in the heat later. The last few kilometres seemed to go on forever, and small things were getting to us. We were finding things hard to handle emotionally, and we hoped our second week wouldn't feel as physically gruelling as the first. We had expected temperatures in the low twenties, which would have been normal at this time of year and might have felt more manageable, but instead we were experiencing day after day of 35 degrees Celsius. We would need to endure these conditions for a while longer yet.

We arrived in Villafranca de los Barros to find a clean and comfortable albergue. Our Canadian friends had signed the visitor book the night before, so we knew we weren't far behind them. We showered then tried to find a café for a cold drink and some tapas to get us by until the restaurants opened and started to serve dinner around eight thirty or nine o'clock.

The town was larger than we had expected and we were surprised to find a row of places open to eat near the main plaza. Pilgrims are often given the *menu de dia* (menu of the day), which generally consists of three courses – for example, chicken noodle soup, a main course of chips with either pork or cod, and a small round baked custard. Today we decided to order from the main menu, and Mike was not able to come to terms with the plate of food that was put in front of him. In truth, he was at the end of his tether today. He vented his anger like a child about lots of things, including the food in front of him. 'I can't eat this crap.'

I sat back feeling emotional and not really knowing what to say to make it better for him or for me. I sat quietly opposite a person who, momentarily, I did not recognise as the gentle man who generally managed most situations well. Everything just felt too hard to cope with. Later I learned that a meal at the end of the day was what he looked forward to most to erase the hardship that had come before it. But now we had to eat something, so we both ate what we could. As funny as it sounds, we needed to get out and go for a walk.

We wandered slowly through the streets and found a small grocery store where we bought a couple of tins of sardines, a breadstick, two apples, two mandarins and water for the next day. Our mood had picked up by now and we began exploring, finding the way out of town for the following morning, given we would be leaving in the dark again.

While exploring, we came upon the Colegio San José, a Jesuit college. It is a grand old building that is also a boarding school for boys. We entered the small foyer and introduced ourselves as pilgrims, had our credentials stamped, and were shown the beautiful and serene chapel. Fernando, one of the trainee priests who spoke some English, gave us a copy of the San José prayer. I asked him if he wouldn't mind translating it for us. We sat in the pews listening to the timeless and comforting words written by Mariano Blanco Fernández, a teacher at the college:

Camino

Senderos de luz hacía la eternidad,
he conocido tu historia,
ahora es momento de recorrer.
Confiar, caminar, orar, crecer,
vivir según tus designios
comprendiendo tus palabras,
encontrarte en mi corazón.
Completar con tus huellas mis pisadas,
sentirte compañero de misión.
Traspasar los límites de mi razón
para poner en Santiago mi morada.
Pararme aquí, mirarte cara a cara
pone a prueba mi fe y mi interior,
me dispone a la batalla
a dejarme abrazar por tu amor.
Tengo ganas de amar, quiero que seas mi consuelo.
Te siento en cada paso que doy y en cada kilómetro resuelto,
por eso mi oración es verso suelto,
reflejo vivo de tu presencia en mi corazón.
Acompáñame, camina conmigo.
¿Mi meta? Santiago. ¿Mi deseo? Abrazarte, Dios.

written by Mariano Blanco Fernández

I Walk

Paths of light to the eternity,
I have known your story,
now it is time to wander.
To trust, walk, pray, grow,
to live according to your designs
understanding your words,
to find you in my heart.
To fill in your footprints with my footsteps,
to feel you as a companion of the mission.
To surpass the limits of reason
to put my dwelling in Santiago.
To stand here, looking at you face to face
testing my faith and my inner being,
setting me on the battlefield
to burn for your love.
I want to love; I want you to be my comforter.
I feel you in every step I take and in every mile complete,
that is why my prayer is a free flow verse,
a living reflection of your presence in my heart.
Accompany me, walk with me.
My goal? Santiago. My wish? To embrace you, God.

written by Mariano Blanco Fernández

My time in the chapel was peaceful and helped me to centre myself once more. I had felt disconnected from my purpose in doing the Camino since beginning a week ago. The challenges I was facing had thrown me off balance in every way possible. I now felt more focused and reconnected to the path ahead.

On returning to the albergue, we met Kieran, a young Irishman, who was poring over his maps with phone in hand, preoccupied with making calculations and taking notes. We introduced ourselves, grabbed a cuppa from the communal kitchen and shared stories from our journey. Kieran had two weeks to make it to Salamanca before flying home to Dublin. He told us how he timed his kilometres and worked out where he planned to be at any particular time. This was in stark contrast to our own planning and I was amazed at how meticulous he was. Meeting Kieran reminded me of times we had come across other pilgrims who spoke English and how great it was to be able to have a conversation and share the journey. I loved their energy, enthusiasm and optimism. I loved listening to their stories; what drew them to walk this Camino; why they were doing it; what sustained them; where they were from; their background and family history; their expectations of their Camino. This sharing, however, was more often about physical and mental experiences than spiritual ones. Maybe that's because we crossed each other's paths only briefly or intermittently. I held back opening up about my spiritual reasons for doing the Camino. I'm not sure why – whether it was because I didn't want people to feel uncomfortable talking about the God thing. It's funny, because for hundreds of years people walked the Camino for religious reasons or for penance. People probably don't walk for penance much these days but the statistics tell us that a lot of people do walk the Camino to find greater meaning or to deepen their spirituality. I wanted to talk about this but was tentative – holding back to sense if the other person was walking it for spiritual reasons too. And yet, I knew that many people did walk this as part of their inner search, I wanted to find these kindred spirits and hear their stories. But I didn't meet many – hardly any. Most of those we met said they did it because they had always wanted to, it was a goal of theirs, they wanted to get fit, wanted to see more of this rustic part of Spain. And yet I wondered…

Perhaps others were feeling similar to me – reluctant to reveal something so personal. If someone asked me directly why I was walking this Camino, I didn't hesitate to say, 'I'm on a spiritual pilgrimage.' Usually the questions stopped there.

We said goodnight to Kieran and signed the visitors' book rather than in the morning to ensure a quick and quiet getaway. Some nights in the albergues were interesting. Generally, everyone was so tired from the day's walking that we all slept reasonably well. However, some nights brought noises that could compete with the wild bush birds of the Murray River of northern Victoria. We were used to people snoring, but on one particular night in the room next to us a guy snored so loudly and incessantly that I was reduced to throwing shoes at the wall in an attempt to wake him or at least make him roll over. I think at one stage I even kicked the wall. I don't remember much after that.

Each morning we started out in the dark, trying not to disturb the sleeping town as boots met stone on the deserted streets. We welcomed the fresh cool air on our faces. The black satin sky was sprinkled with silver sequins, which bewitched and befriended us as we edged our way to the outskirts of the town, each with our own separate thoughts of what challenges, insights and learning await us on this new day. We hoped and prayed that it would be only minutes before we would find a café open for our morning ritual of *tostadas* and *café con leche*. We had already noticed that there was no takeaway coffee to be found anywhere. Not that we wanted one, but we couldn't help noticing the lack of paper cups and plastic lids, which are ubiquitous back home. This is great for the environment but I'm not sure that is the reason for their absence. In rural Spain, if you want a coffee then you sit at the bar, usually alongside your workmates and friends. The morning coffee ritual is very much a time of community, although in some very small towns there is no café or shop at all.

Today our destination was Torremejía, 28 kilometres away along a straight and stony dirt road. I found the flatness of the terrain tedious and numbing, and

I was conscious that I seemed to be whinging a lot. I wished it wasn't so. We had started out this morning two hours earlier than the Spanish walkers, yet they caught up with us around the halfway mark.

At one point, we sighted a single lonely tree about ten metres off the road, which we headed for to sit in some shade only to find that the long dead grass underneath it was dense with prickle bushes. There was no way we could sit on the ground so we sat on our backpacks, but as we sat down, the end of my scarf, which I'd looped around my face and neck to keep the sun off, caught on the prickles. I had to separate myself from the bush by unravelling the other end of the scarf and leaving it there, as it wasn't possible to untangle it from the thorny barbs that were ready to claim another unsuspecting victim. Our shoes, socks and pants were covered in burrs.

As we stood up to put our packs on, Kieran spotted us from a distance, waved and waited. We trod warily around the burrs and thorns as we made our way back to the road. It was wonderful to see him and to feel his young energy and vitality that felt infectious. We walked alongside him for a couple of kilometres, and when we could no longer keep up with his pace, he was off. His watch had broken during his Camino, and its new replacement had stopped just before he'd seen us. We watched our little white rabbit disappear into the distance, determined to make it to Salamanca by his deadline. We didn't see him again, but Lea and Dan caught up with him in Cáceres and he was on schedule.

Walking the Meseta, day after day, was definitely mind-numbing. In my stupor, I became aware of how deep I needed to dig into my resolve just to put one foot in front of the other. My mind was playing games with me. Normally, my mind has plenty to think about and just gets on with its daily tasks, but out here in the never-never it was at a loss to understand its role. Thoughts came and went, and then, nothing. It was like the line on a heart monitor when it flat-lines. Then there was a surge of busyness when my mind started scanning, as if trying to tune into a station on the radio. Bingo, it found a station! It had churned up a memory from long ago that may have been triggered by the heat.

I was a small child sandwiched between two adults in the front of a huge truck. On one side of me was a man who was driving. He was wearing a singlet and shorts and sweating a lot. On my other side was my mother, her brown curls flattened against her perspiring face as she nursed my younger sister on her lap. I was staring down at the white leather sandals on my feet that stuck straight out in front of me. My dress had rolled up at the back and my legs were sweaty against the seat. The driver had said it was a hot day to be moving house and asked Mum if her husband would be meeting her at the new home after he finished work. She nodded, too suffocated by the humidity to utter a word.

We finally arrived at the new house and peeled ourselves from the ridges in the old cracked seats. I was lifted down from the sauna of the truck cabin to the footpath. I squinted against the sun and scanned the street which was a line of red dirt in both directions. I walked past the burgundy-coloured tin letterbox, down the short path, up the few wooden steps to the small front porch and stood at the front door admiring its shiny green paint. I remember thinking that I loved the smell of the new wood and I felt excited to be walking through that door for the first time.

It was the late 1950s, and we had been living in a war service house in Enoggera, a suburb of Brisbane. The new house was on the north side in Brighton, not far from the beach. Little did I know that within a couple of years the Bee Gees would be living just a few kilometres away on the other side of the Hornibrook Highway. A few children about the same age as me stood near the letterbox and shouted out that they had been in my house before me and had climbed all over it while it was being built. They were to become my friends, but at the time, and being five years old, I felt sad that I wasn't the first to explore it.

Forty-eight years later, after the death of my father in 2005, my husband and I walked up those front steps to meet the current owners. I gave them some background information on the house and our family, and explained that where the established estate is now there had been nothing but red dirt, cane toads, snakes and mango trees. Beyond the considerable backyard lay sugar cane fields, and at the end of the street was a wonderful swamp with bushland. They didn't seem too interested. I asked if I could take a quick look through the house but they had just acquired a new music system and the lounge-room floor was covered in equipment. They said I could take a wander around the backyard. The mango tree still stood along with the swing Dad had built us so long ago.

The concrete square where the back path came to an abrupt halt sat vacant as a reminder of where the old dunny had once stood. As a child, one of my chores on Saturday mornings was to cut up the *Courier Mail* newspaper into squares, put a hole through one of the corners, thread string through the holes, tie a knot and hang the paper on a nail on the wall of the toilet. This was our toilet paper. I would fill the sawdust box and sweep the toilet out. I also hung a small round air freshener on another wall, piercing the paper to allow the scent of rose or lavender to escape.

Mike videoed me narrating stories in the backyard and in the street. With a tear in my eye we passed by the house where my best girlfriend had lived; she died at the age of 32. I recounted some stories to the camera of all our antics as we grew up in that street. We chased horses in the back paddock, saved wild bush wallabies from the local dogs, caught tadpoles for school nature programs, weaved golden silk from silkworms, fell out of mango trees into prickly pear bushes (afterwards I was thrown across Mrs Eckersley's laminated kitchen table to have my backside tweezered), danced to the Bee Gees and the Beatles on our record players, heard JFK was shot, sewed outfits on the Singer sewing machine for the next Saturday's dance, protested the Vietnam War, grew up and left it behind.

It was now mid-October and some of the accommodation along the Camino was closing down because there were fewer pilgrims on the path at this time of year. We arrived early at the village of Aljucén after a relatively short walk of 18 kilometres from Mérida. We decided to stop to eat lunch before finding a place to stay, which was unusual – we would normally arrive in a town after 2 pm when everything was shut for siesta. There was only one bar and fortunately it was open. The lighting was dim and the room had a scattering of tables and plastic outdoor chairs; behind the bar was a huge picture of the New York skyline.

After we'd ordered, a fellow pilgrim walked in. '*Hola!*' we called out as he sat at another table. He was jolly-looking, in his sixties we guessed, with a round-faced smile. We recognised him as the snoring man who'd kept me awake the other night and whose nocturnal symphony had shaken the foundations of the albergue. Mike and I looked at each in dismay. What if we had to share a space again tonight? Could our nerves handle another performance like that? We discussed the option of getting out on the road again and walking on to the next town, a further 17 kilometres, but if we had a golden rule, it was to not push ourselves too far and risk injury. But we had made good time, we told ourselves, and it was still early afternoon. We could do it! Feeling invincible, we set out with a spring in our step on to Alcuéscar.

The route from Aljucén to Alcuéscar was made up of sandy tracks, dry riverbeds and flat gravelly paths that weaved between thick scrubland and bushy trees standing at eye level. With our view not extending more than a few metres, it felt claustrophobic. Towards the end, the route rose up to a saddle and then descended onto hard gravel paths that changed to bitumen roads on the outskirts of the town. For most of it, we were walking in the late afternoon, the hottest time of the day. The combination of the heat and the hard featureless landscape meant this was one of our hardest legs. We saw no animals and almost no people except once on a narrow trail when we had to squeeze to the side to make room for a 4WD coming towards us out of the scrub. As it passed, we didn't have the energy to wave to the family in the air-conditioned Range Rover. We exchanged blank looks with the parents and their kids in the back seat, as if none of us had expected to see another person on this desolate stretch.

We reached the saddle as the light was fading. After not having had any perspective of the landscape, we were able to look back on the range of mountains. Mike marvelled at the deep red colours of the sunset. I could see it was beautiful but I couldn't have cared less in that moment. By the end of the afternoon, the nerve pain in my leg was excruciating. I could focus only on carrying myself those last few kilometres and being able to lie down. We could see the town in the distance; it couldn't be far away now. Then it would disappear for what seemed like ages and reappear, taunting us for a few more kilometres. We had discussed this phenomenon with other pilgrims and they all had their own experience of this. We could laugh later, but at the time it was frustrating and almost torturous.

We entered Alcuéscar on dusk where we found the monastery that housed the albergue mentioned in our guidebook. The friendly American manager was half expecting us as the other pilgrims had mentioned that the Australians might still be coming. She showed us to the cell where we would sleep. This was the last night of the season, she told us, and from tomorrow the albergue section of the monastery would be closed. For dinner, she suggested the bar across the road. It was now almost eight o'clock and the doors to the monastery would be locked at nine. Dinner with the monks had been served much earlier, and there was nothing left to offer us, she apologised.

Heading down the driveway we were stopped by a man who needed assistance to get across the highway to the café-bar. Weary as we were, and with nothing much to give emotionally, the man grabbed my hand and held it while Mike pushed him in his wheelchair. Apparently, he was a 'frequent flyer' at the bar. We ordered him a *café con leche* and he started to stroke my hand. He motioned to Mike to leave – Mike was ruining his romantic moment. For me, it was humorous but at the same time I felt uncomfortable, not knowing how to handle it. Mike patiently asked if he could have his wife back. After I gently rebuffed his repeated gestures of affection, he appeared content to focus on his cup of coffee. Then he waved goodbye and greeted the locals, whom he obviously knew.

The waitress dropped menus on the table for us and we let her know we would need to leave in 20 minutes to get back to the monastery so we wouldn't be locked out. The menu was the most disappointing yet. An egg and some chips would have to do, and of course a glass of red to wash it down. We were learning to adjust our expectations and not to look forward to a hearty meal at the end of the day in rural areas. The cities have much more to offer, but in the countryside the menus and nutrition are pretty limited. Two things that were consistently good, however, were the coffee and the red wine, both of which we could not – would not – have done without. They were our rewards for a hard day's work. Other pilgrims laughed when we drank only one glass of wine each. 'Why aren't you drinking?' they would say, as if one glass didn't count. They could all drink us under the table and still be good to go the next morning without any apparent hangover.

As we were about to leave, the staff at the bar told us our new friend would be taken back to his home, which was in a separate building on the same property as the monastery. We arrived back to find a group sitting in lounge chairs all speaking in Spanish. We would have loved to join in for a while to connect with others in conversation, but they didn't speak any English and we had no conversational Spanish, so we had a shower and went off to bed. Mike lay down on his bunk in the cell, and crack! – he hit the floor. Some of the slats under the thin mattress had broken. It would be another interesting and uncomfortable night, but we were so hot and tired it was lights out.

The next morning my leg was killing me and Mike's back was giving him grief. We were paying for having broken our cardinal rule. Other pilgrims were busy packing up and talking about catching the bus. What bus? The manager said everyone except one person would be taking the bus the 33 kilometres into the city of Cáceres this morning, and we could tag along if we wanted to. At about 8 am, as a group, we simultaneously heaved our packs onto our shoulders, strapped up, filled our water bottles and made our way down the stairs, around the courtyard and out on to the street. We said goodbye to the one brave soul who set off on a dirt track to walk the 33 kilometres in what was promising to be a day of searing heat. From under the brim of my hat I glanced up, squinting at the cloudless blue sky, and already I could feel the heat upon my face.

The manager must have noticed me as she said, 'It's going to be another one of those intense hot ones.'

I felt guilty at not being able to make the distance to Cáceres and felt a little anxious. I would deal with this later. It was quite novel walking with others up the footpath single-file like a row of ducks, past the bar where we had shared a drink with our amorous friend the night before, past white-washed stone houses and a fruit and vegetable store to the bus stop. The locals stared. Except for meeting Lea and Dan and experiencing the odd encounter at an albergue, we had spent most of our days on our own since Seville. It felt good to be among others and experience the connection of the Camino, whether we knew them or not.

We piled on the bus and sat behind a girl in her early thirties who introduced herself as Olga from Barcelona. She was about to finish her Camino in Cáceres and would stay there for a few days before returning to her job. Compared to most of the Spaniards we met, her colouring was fair and she spoke English very well.

Once we left Alcuéscar behind, I sat back and looked out at the flat, dry, barren landscape. As the kilometres sped by, I realised we would arrive in Cáceres in no time. It was difficult to make sense of being on a bus. This was an unplanned 'day off' and normally it would have been a long, hot day of walking. I felt despondent but I knew the decision to take the bus was the right one.

As a Catalan, Olga spoke of how the people of Catalonia regarded themselves as independent from the rest of Spain, both culturally and politically. In fact, the next year, in late 2017, Catalonia declared itself an independent republic. We also talked about the Camino – about how isolating it could be, our injuries, and why we were catching the bus. Olga asked whether we knew Cáceres and where we would find medical help. We said we had no idea but would work it out. She offered to walk us to a clinic she knew and to speak to the receptionist for us. We were so appreciative.

When we arrived in the city and Olga found the medical clinic, the staff at reception said the doctor couldn't see us because we weren't Spanish citizens and there were complications with using our travel insurance. We would need to go to the hospital. The three of us walked from the newer section of the city to the older part where bitumen roads gave way to cobblestone streets.

There are many layers to Cáceres – first, the modern tree-lined avenues with designer shops and businesses, and then the older area with ornate buildings and a central plaza featuring a large area of decoratively patterned stonework. The plaza meets seamlessly with the next layer, the ancient wall that surrounds the medieval city within. The first time I walked up those stone steps and stepped through one of the original archways, I was transported into another time. I marvelled at its splendour, its history and its authenticity – it was perfectly preserved (no crumbling ruins here!). It was like being cast in *Game of Thrones* (many of its scenes were filmed on location here) or *Camelot*.

I was excited to be in a city more than 1,100 years old – Australia has none older than 220.[4] The only other historic large city we had experienced on the Camino so far was Mérida. Walking across the Roman bridge entering Mérida, I was really surprised at how overwhelmed I felt encountering traffic and crowds of people. It was wonderful to arrive there, to rest and to experience the energy, but after a day, I also wanted to escape and return to the solitude of the Camino once more.

In Cáceres, Olga had booked a room nearby, so we gave each other a hug and parted company to find our own accommodation. Given my pain and this being a large city, we decided not to stay in an albergue, so we booked into a small apartment owned by a hotel further down the street. It was modern, comfortable and central, and the *urgencias* (emergency department) was not too far away.

We found our way to the hospital where I needed to show my passport and travel insurance documents. I was triaged by a couple of nurses and told to sit

---

[4] I mean cities under 'white settlement' – we have of course had sophisticated civilisations as old as 60,000 years.

and wait, but it wasn't long before I was taken to see the doctor, a middle-aged Spanish woman wearing an old-fashioned white button-through coat, her hair rolled under at the ends like a 1960s style. She was welcoming in a matter-of-fact way.

I was able to make myself understood via the doctor's computer, which despite being ancient, featured a translation function. The doctor typed in Spanish, and it translated into English. I then typed my answer in English and it translated to Spanish. This took a little while, but I found her patient, respectful and genuinely interested in fully understanding my complaint. She prescribed anti-inflammatories and painkillers and asked about my blisters. I told her that I had them covered because I'd visited a podiatrist a couple of times before leaving home and knew how to lance and disinfect my wounds, apply saline and dress them with bandages. My pack was certainly heavier with the saline pouches.

I think she was impressed – but that was the only part of my self-care she was impressed with. She examined my legs, which were covered in a deep red and purple rash from below my knees to my ankles. I was told the rash was caused by a combination of heat, friction and circulation problems from pushing myself beyond my limit, for which she prescribed a cortisone cream. She also sent me to a physio, who was fabulous and suggested that I take a few days to rest from the Camino. I felt guilty for taking the extra time, but I took her advice.

For a year prior to leaving to walk the Camino, I was seeing a physio on a regular basis for nerve pain in my lower back area which radiated into my left leg. I could hear the physio's voice, 'If you are determined to walk this Camino, you will suffer.'

I replied, 'Yes, I know, but I'm going to do it anyway.'

'The path' had taken on a powerful life of its own. My self-discipline and sense of commitment to the journey were overriding good-reason, and my health and wellbeing were suffering. In the midst of this extraordinary historical city, all I could envisage were my feet treading the path ahead. I wanted to be back on the pilgrimage again. I was feeling off-track and restless. This was not how I had envisaged it would be. What had happened to the peace, serenity and contemplation?

Then there was the guilt trip. I needed to backtrack to make up those kilometres we had lost taking the bus. What would people think if I didn't? Would it be cheating? I'd told everyone I would walk the whole way. No, I had to go back, and so the pressure was on. I could ignore my pain – yep, that would work; mind over matter and all of that.

Mike didn't share my feelings. 'Let it go. It's only 33 kilometres out of 1006 – let yourself off the hook. Let's spend some days enjoying this city. Let's go have a beer.'

When I'm feeling like this, Mike jokes about a character he invented called Hector. One day he drew me a cartoon of a hamster on a wheel.

'Meet Hector,' he said. 'That's what your brain is doing!'

He was pointing out my perfectionist side. I couldn't allow myself to rest until the job was done.

From time to time he would say, 'Sounds like Hector is pretty busy on that wheel today.'

Mike found a souvenir shop that sold magnets of children's names and we found a 'Hector' one for me. The magnet now sits on our fridge at home as a reminder.

At the beginning of the Camino, Mike and I made a commitment to ourselves to walk for seven days and then rest up in a bigger town for two nights where we would take it easy, do some washing, and have access to a better variety and quality of food. Cáceres seemed an ideal place for such a break. The next day was our wedding anniversary, which was another good reason to stay put.

We were happy to run into Lea and Dan in the city too; they'd been resting and were about to move on the next day. We shared a great meal and a bottle of wine together. The next day Mike bought some walking pants and a shirt, and we did some sightseeing – it was a good day spent relaxing and indulging, just as we often do on a weekend at home. After two nights, I was feeling much better and had itchy feet to get back on the track again.

We started out the following morning, enjoying the thought of a shorter walk of only 16 kilometres to the next town, Casar de Cáceres. We had established a routine where we would stop on the outskirts of town after walking for an hour or so, take off our packs and stretch our backs. Today, while we stretched, Mike's back began to spasm and he could hardly move with the pain. He dropped to the ground on his hands and knees.

Mike

It was hard getting into the rhythm of walking when the terrain was flat and the discomfort of the heat made it difficult to appreciate the natural surroundings. It looked interesting to begin with, but after days of feeling overheated, exhausted and sore, all the details seemed to blur or become less important than getting to the end of our day's journey. The miles of stonewalls that bordered some of the farms were no more than an interesting feature at first, but then they gave us relief at certain times of the day because they provided shade when we sat down and rested against them.

Behind the walls we occasionally saw black pigs foraging for acorns under the oak trees. There were lots of trees and they were always the same: oak trees, olive trees and cork trees. In a moment of rest, I asked Google about the land and trees of this region. The type of oak trees here are called holm oaks and native to the Mediterranean. They are known for their hardiness in harsh conditions and once they become established in an area, they are virtually indestructible. The fallen acorns are eaten by the black pigs. It is the acorns that give *jamón ibérico* its special flavour.

During this time in Extremadura we saw and heard more dogs than people. Curious animals were the only witnesses to our walking the long stretches between villages. In the countryside, it was common to see dogs on their own or in pairs guarding a property or a herd of goats. In the industrial estates on the edge of towns, I saw occasional stray dogs, including in one case a thin black Labrador, who watched us tentatively from a distance. I felt sad because of its poor physical condition – I left bread on a rock where the dog could see it. One morning we walked through a farm and were surrounded by a herd of goats with long floppy ears and pendulous udders. Instead of a goat-herder, there was a dog minding them. He looked like a Great Dane and came to greet us with wagging tail and smiling eyes, aching to be patted and to have his ears fondled. Meeting him brought out our playful side and we talked to the dog and hugged him like he was a big puppy. After repeating, 'Who's a good boy then? Who's a good shepherd? Yes, you are!' we said goodbye and felt our spirits buoyed.

When walking through the towns, I was curious about the homes, which mostly had a Mediterranean feel to them. The first thing you notice about houses in Extremadura is that they have been built to withstand the harsh climate. Out front there was often a wooden door, always solidly constructed, almost fortified, to withstand the centuries, or perhaps the blows from the rifle butts and boots of Franco's secret police. In some of the more well-off homes, the doors were elegant with beautifully crafted brass or iron door-knockers depicting an animal or a small hand knocking. Most buildings were constructed of solid whitewashed stone, with white-tiled floors to help to keep the interior cool. Occasionally we walked past a house where the door was ajar and we could see into the interior, or into a courtyard lush with greenery and brightly coloured flowers of a well-cared-for garden. Once I saw an elegant table and chair with an open bottle of wine next to a plate of food waiting to be eaten. It looked as perfect as a still life painting.

The physical environment and the climate here are tough, and for many people life is hard. But on the other side of many doors that we pass, there's often a world of exquisite beauty hidden from outsiders like us.

On one of these days, I reflected on the prayer we had read at the Colegio San José in Villafranca de los Barros a few days earlier. It was a prayer to the *peregrino* and it read in part:

To stand here, looking at you face to face
Testing my faith and my inner being…

I thought about that reference to my 'inner being' and Dan's comment came back to me: 'You will have lots of time to explore every nook and cranny of your mind…'

I was disappointed that my interior seemed entirely barren, and my biggest spiritual challenge was boredom. I seemed to have spent a lot of time thinking about projects I would undertake when I returned home. I started planning a new water tank and thought about re-plumbing the toilet to make use of the water it would store. I thought about my business. Many a time I created a balance sheet of my assets and the amount of money I would need for my 'retirement' one day. I started to imagine what retirement might look like. That was too hard and so I reviewed the break-even costs of my business and thought of ways I could reduce my overheads and whether it was worth employing people or hiring contractors to help me deliver more services. My old *compadres*, Señors Anxiety and Worry frequently dropped in to keep me company. We talked about my business floundering on the rocks of bankruptcy while I walked through the countryside in Spain happily unaware of the taxation office's final letter of demand for payment. They both become frequent companions on the long empty stretches.

'Hola, Señor Miguel. The news is not good today, I am afraid.'

'Oh, you again. What is it this time?'

'We were just wondering if you had considered your responsibilities back home while you are doing this Camino.'

'I'm not talking to you today.'

'I hope your dinner is better tonight than the meal you were served last night – we know how disappointed you were. We tried to tell you.'

'Are you still here…?'

'Si, Señor, we would not dream of leaving you alone on these long empty stretches.'

86

We were in the middle of a vast winemaking district in Extremadura and there was lots of activity as we passed acres and acres of vineyards. It was harvest time and there was an urgency to get the grapes to the next stage of production before they spoiled in the heat. We saw trails of dust in the distance signalling a convoy of trucks, tractors and Renault vans all pulling trailers of harvested grapes to be crushed and processed.

Once, we stepped off the road as one of these road trains passed us. As we shielded our faces from the dust, the driver of the last tractor in the convoy slowed down and waved to us to climb onto the trailer and help ourselves to a bunch of grapes. He came to a stop and I climbed onto the wheel and hauled myself up to grab a handful of grapes from the huge trailer. Stepping down, I waved him a thank you. The driver, not satisfied with the size of my takings, put the tractor into park and climbed up on the trailer to find a larger bunch of grapes for us. He washed it with the contents of his drinking bottle and handed it to me, laughing and chatting in Spanish before waving and shouting 'Buen Camino!'

When I wasn't thinking about water tanks, plumbing the toilet and the bottom line of my business, my thoughts ranged randomly across past friendships and relationships. I remembered people in primary school and those I had lost touch with in high school. I recalled Michael Burns in Grade three who often got me in trouble for making me laugh at his imitation of Miss Hickey's story-time sessions (she had a gravelly voice from smoking too many cigarettes and Michael made her sound like Deadly Earnest from the Late Show).

I relived billy cart races down the perilous Dorothy Street hill and how the sharp bend at the bottom often ended in tears, splintered wood, and scraped knees and elbows. I thought about old girlfriends who had once lit a fire in my heart. As I leafed back through the pages of my past, I pondered why so many romantic chapters had ended the way they had. I remember a friend describing to me how he still keeps in touch with most of his old girlfriends. He has even had dinner with them from time to time and exchanges birthday greetings. This was astonishing to me and I remember telling him that if I ever caught up with my old flames now, I would be lucky if I got away with just a slap in the face. Was it my insensitivity? This troubled me for many days. It was confronting, but I had to admit for a few years there, I have not always acted out of loving kindness towards those who have been close to me or loved me.

I remembered my father. He first met Cici for the first time while in hospital wearing his blue dressing gown. A year later he entered palliative care. We spent some afternoons pushing him in his wheelchair in Box Hill Park, where once he said to Cici, 'I haven't always looked this way you know.' I tried to make up for not having spent much time with him since I left home.

I recalled the most exciting thing when I was small was going to work with Dad one day in his Ford and walking beside him while he carried his toolbox across the factory floor, the air buzzing with the sound of high-speed machinery. I remembered how he would also polish my shoes on Sunday nights when I was in primary school. That was his way of saying, 'I love you'. Towards the end he was profoundly sad that the cancer had cheated him of his final years and his chance to travel once again (perhaps to Spain once more). Whereas my mum's death was simple and sudden (a stroke), it was like her spirit had flown free from its cage, whereas my dad's was a lingering, lonely and undignified finale.

One night in the albergue it was hard to fall sleep because of these memories. It was also compounded by the distractions of the insomniac in the next bunk. A bluish light emanated from his phone as he studied his Facebook page into the early hours, while I tossed and turned.

Yes indeed, you have lots of time on the Camino to think about the big questions of life.

Over the years I have built up a small library including a modest collection of popular philosophy. I read a couple of these books specifically in preparation for the Camino so that I could digest and reflect on them during the long days and nights. One was a meditation by Gordon Livingston, a veteran psychiatrist of many decades, who summed up his life's lessons in his book *Too Soon Old, Too Late Smart*. He described his philosophy on living a contented life with these words: 'The three components of contentment are something to do, someone to love, and something to look forward to.'

While I was doing pretty well so far on the second ingredient (someone to love), I had problems relating to the first (something to do) and the third (something to look forward to). Walking the Camino is technically 'something to do', but here was the problem: it no longer engaged me. I have loved walking in the past. Walking with Cici in preparation for the Camino was enjoyable and left me feeling excited in anticipation of the adventure. We had now been walking more than ten days and I had not felt anything similar to the pleasure of our training walks.

As for 'something to look forward to', this had been the most disappointing aspect of all. What was there to look forward to at the end of the day? I had expected a cosy pension in a little village, a delicious meal followed by a pleasant night's sleep in a comfy bed feeling the satisfaction of having completed a challenging but rewarding day of walking. There was none of that so far. Perhaps it was due to my lack of clear purpose for being here.

For centuries pilgrims walked 'the Way' for reasons of atonement, self-realisation, or being closer to God. Cici, like those pilgrims before us, drew inspiration from things like a blessing written to *peregrinos* on the wall of an albergue, or a small hand-made crucifix she discovered left on the road. For her, the crucifix was a 'sign'. There was a lot of the 'spiritual' in her experiences that seemed to give her a strong purpose and strength. I didn't have that spiritual view on things. For me, the reason the cross was there on the road was commonplace and distinctly unspiritual: 'Someone has lost it. Or maybe they just threw it away because they got a better one'. (I remember Cici frowned when I suggested this).

While Cici's motivation for this pilgrimage is loftier than mine, I keep trying to work out my own. Surely it wasn't only to support her on the journey. Yet I didn't know what was driving me to get through the long monotonous days. I seriously considered what my true goal was and whether I even had one. When did I last pursue a goal with the sort of determination like my wife's? I remembered my early years and my short-lived career as a corporate lawyer. How stressful and often boring that all was, especially my days in court listening to technical arguments that made me struggle to stay awake. I was motivated to just get through it. This thought had a clear ring of truth to it. Maybe that was it. The scary thing is that so much of what I did in life seemed to be driven by that singular motivation. It bothered me that I couldn't think of a better reason for doing this bloody walk than to just get through it.

What appealed to me when I started preparing for this trek was the idea of having so much time that, for once, I could feel in control. In my normal life, many days feel like a battle with time. Life on the Camino is life made simple – or it should be. There is just one task, to walk from the town we woke up in and arrive at the town where we will rest our heads at night. It sounded like bliss. There would be no distractions, no emails, no phone calls and no juggling of tasks – just one thing to do after another. Time wouldn't overwhelm me. Instead, I imagined, the passage of time would be like grains of sand in an hourglass lining up one after another to tumble from the top part into the bottom part – all unhurried and orderly.

Here's what actually happens at the start of each day. Waking up in the dark I am conscious only of thinking: *how many kilometres are there to cover today? Where will we be when the sun is at its zenith at two o'clock? Will we have reached the town by then?* We carefully pack our bedding, head torches and toiletries into our backpacks without turning on the lights so we don't wake the other walkers who are still slumbering. Usually, we are the first out the dormitory door. We quietly make our way down the dark stairs carrying our boots under our arms. We pause in the vestibule to gather our walking poles, again trying not to disturb our sleeping *compadres*. As we fiddle with the lock and the door, I try to remember which street we need to follow to return to the path on the edge of town. Hopefully there will be a café on the way where we can pause briefly and begin to wake up. We are outside in the bracing cold air under an inky sky trying to orientate ourselves, in whispers, to the direction of the way out of town. I pause to take a deep breath. It begins again…

It's surprising how much time I spend thinking about food. After a few weeks, I wrote in my journal: '*Mea culpa*! Forgive me! This is going to be a rant. I need to vent! What is becoming the most challenging part of our grand adventure in rural Spain is not the long hours of walking each day, it isn't even the pain I inflict upon myself and then manage with anti-inflammatories and painkillers, it's the food.'

When walking in the heat, and then later in the freezing rain, I looked forward to something nice at the end of the day – specifically a nice meal. Good food energises me for the day's challenges and it is a reward for the pain, heat, aches and boredom that is endured. But unlike Cici, my lack of spiritual perspective made it hard to just go with the flow. For me, the culinary aspect of my adventure in Extremadura and Andalusia was hard on the palate (and the spirit). The food was very basic and it is generally the same wherever you go.[5] (In hindsight, I realise our choice was severely limited by our lack of local knowledge and working Spanish).

I don't know what constitutes 'true' Spanish food. In my ignorance, I conjured up plates of paella and tapas. So far, we have not come across either of these except in Seville, Mérida and later, in the region of Galicia. Most of our meals consisted of cod or (sometimes) trout, fried egg and chips, croquettes (filled with pork and cheese or blood sausage), cheese (usually a hard white variety similar to the Italian Pecorino Romano but not as flavoursome), tortilla (omelette with potatoes), or pork. Yes, with pork there was variety – fried pork, suckling pig, pig trotters, chorizo, pig ears, pig tails, dried pig's blood and even, in some parts, dried pig faces, which could be found hanging, like Halloween masks, on the walls of delis. Then of course, there is *jamón*, cured and thinly sliced pork. The best quality, which the Spanish people love especially, comes from Iberian pigs fed on acorns. Jamón is as Spanish as El Cid and bullfighting. When it comes to jamón, they enjoy it with everything.

Order a trout – it's stuffed with jamón. Order a salad – there's jamón on the side. If you order a cheese sandwich, they will ask, 'Do you want jamón with that?'

'No, thank you.'

'Are you sure? No jamón?'

For vegetarians like Cici, the prospect of finishing a day of walking and approaching a restaurant can bring on a bout of anxiety. As a general rule, meals are not served with salads or sides of vegetables. Menus are noticeably lacking when it comes to anything that is green or has grown in the ground (apart from chips).

One night, we asked the waitress if it was possible to have vegetables with our salt cod '*¿Es posible tomer…?*'; ('Is it possible…?') '*No, no es posible…*';

---

[5] The Vía de la Plata has far less foreign *peregrinos* and so tends not to cater for them like the Camino Francés.

('*No, it's not...*'). To be fair, we did have a wonderful bean stew in Monesterio, the *jamón* capital of Spain. And later we ate some delicious grilled peppers – without *jamón*. I forgot to mention that it is common in larger towns to find the uniquely Spanish salad known as *ensalada mixta*. This is usually the cheapest item on the menu, at two or three euros, because, it seems, the least thought and effort goes into its preparation. It's basically finely chopped iceberg lettuce, thinly sliced tomato, a few bits of green pepper and some chunks of onion. No dressing, though maybe some olive oil. It often comes with tinned tuna. There's also a 'deluxe' version of *ensalada mixta*, which comes with – yes, some slices of *jamón*.

We have walked about six kilometres since leaving the ancient city of Cáceres and are one third of the way to the next town, Casar de Cáceres. The road passes through landscape that is flat and featureless though the sky is blue and boundless. Having rested up for those days in Cáceres, it is turning out to be a surprisingly pleasant walk! Soon the landscape changes to tall grasslands swaying with the wind and we walk along millennia-old Roman roads. We change our gait and start marching, swinging our arms and imagining ourselves as legionnaires. Cici takes the lead position, repeating 'Hup, two, three, four!' We march for a couple of kilometres before seeing a figure in the distance. He is a German pilgrim walking with his dog, a kelpie. We chat briefly before moving on. A few moments later I turn to look back at our companion but he has disappeared. A phantom *peregrino*!

In the middle of these beautiful fields, we stop to make a short video. Cici faces my camera and talks about the town we have just left. She looks across the fields, which she describes as the Elysian Fields, perhaps because she is thinking of that scene in the film *Gladiator* where Maximus pushes open the door to eternity and is confronted by his beloved fields of wheat. We rest for 10 or 15 minutes. I do a few stretches, bending forwards, tilting at the hips, simple stretches that I have done hundreds of times before – and then it happens. Just as I swing my pack on, a pain shoots through my back. It is indescribable. My lower back muscles spasm and I can no longer stand up. The breathing! Stop panting,

I tell myself, and breathe slowly, regularly. In a moment, I am down on my hands and knees on the ground, unclipping my pack. Cici is alarmed. 'What is it? What is it?'

'Give me a minute,' I tell her as I try to slow my breathing. I am unable to straighten up. I realise within a few moments that I cannot walk. I have had twinges in my back since that day we pushed ourselves to walk 35 kilometres to Alcuéscar. Since then my body has sent me a warning message every so often, a twinge here or a sharp pain there, which I have ignored. Today my body and my subconscious have decided on a new strategy: 'We need to give him something he'll really pay attention to.'

After ten minutes of feeling dizzy and nauseous, I am able to get to my feet. We have to move on. Cici helps me on with my pack. After a couple of hours of limping and hobbling with frequent stops and lots of expletives when I stumble or stub my toe on a rock, we see Casar de Cáceres on the horizon.

Unlike Cáceres, Casar de Cáceres is a small town. The way in is via a wide two-lane highway with little to look at on either side of the road except factories, goats, the usual barking, snarling dogs and lots of small farms littered with rusting farm equipment. The smell of pig excrement is on the breeze. It is here on this barren stretch of road that we meet the enigmatic traveller Sasha, who appears as a solitary figure staring down the highway. To look at him, you would think he was homeless. My first thought was *This poor man needs help!* He stood alone like a person shipwrecked on an island. Instead of a backpack, he carried a battered suitcase with a bucket handle, its weight on his shoulder cushioned by a folded towel. As soon as he saw us, he smiled and welcomed us in Russian.

Sasha was from Siberia, and he had spent the past four months criss-crossing Spain on foot. He knew no Spanish, which was quite a remarkable feat for someone who had spent that length of time here. He spoke no English either, except for a very few words, including 'good' and 'super good' (extremely good). He was adept at using sign language and making sound effects to get his point across – for example, he would whistle and roll his eyes to describe something or someone as very crazy or a lot of fun. Via translation apps, he told us he was a journalist and was searching for something in Spain – but this bit was vague.

When we arrived on the outskirts of town, Sasha pointed to a café and announced in English, 'Let's do business lunch!' We happily paid for his meal, assuming he was penniless, and tried to fill in some of the gaps in his story. Was he actually a *peregrino*? Why was he in this remote part of Spain and where was he headed? Slowly his story unfolded. He told us he was travelling with no particular destination in mind. A year before he had attended a group hypnotherapy session in Moscow where he had learned that he had lived in this part of the world in a previous life. He was now returning to the Spanish plains in search of his home.

After lunch, we continued on to the town square. I was hoping to find some anti-inflammatories and painkillers at a *farmacia* (pharmacy). I was therefore keen to find the main bar in town. The most important thing we had learned so far is that the bartender in the main bar knows everything. He knows the answers to the many questions and dilemmas of peregrinos: the best albergue, where to eat, where not to eat, where to buy food for the next day and most importantly, where to get painkillers.

Another long and painful couple of kilometres of walking brought us to the small town square where we found the local watering hole. The patrons were sitting on stools looking bored, watching football on the TV, and drinking *cerveza*. They had no interest in a few *peregrinos*. The barman unfortunately could not enlighten us on the whereabouts of the nearest open *farmacia* and instead pointed us towards the albergue across the square. It was closed, so we waited on the steps for it to reopen after siesta. It turned out to be one of the more basic ones. In the communal sleeping area, the bunks were pushed close together with barely enough room to walk between them. The façade looked neglected and in need of a new paint job. In many towns, there was little or no money to upgrade the facilities. Inside there was a notice with a list of 'don'ts', which included instructing *peregrinos* not to hang washing to dry outside the windows because it would reflect poorly on the standards of the albergue.

Cici returned from a walk to confirm that there were no pharmacies in town, so we went out for dinner with Sasha – the predictable cod, *ensalada mixta* and good wine. When we returned to the albergue, we discovered that two Spanish cyclists had arrived and unpacked their panniers, covering the one communal table with their supplies. They appeared engrossed in their stocktake and uninterested in making conversation. There was no heating, and there was nothing to do but climb into our sleeping bags and settle down for the night. The windows had heavy wooden shutters in place of glass panes, and when we bolted them closed it felt as though we'd been transported back several centuries to an old inn.

It was one of the worst nights I have experienced – the pain, the hard, uncomfortable beds and the nocturnal groans, snores and other noises of the (almost all male) communal bunk room made it hard to drift off. I frequently woke up in the night and tried to roll over to relieve the pain. Each time I did, I saw Sasha sitting up in bed busily texting on his phone. The town hall clock across from the square struck every half hour and the night passed slowly.

Eventually, the soft blue light of morning penetrated through the thin gaps in the shutters. Slowly and painfully I manoeuvred myself out of the bunk. Walking to the toilet, I could not stand up straight – the pain was so bad – and I needed to brace myself by hanging onto the walls. When I returned, it took us only a moment to assess my situation and make a decision.

We had planned to continue that day to Cañaveral, 33 kilometres away, but we didn't know what kind of medical facilities existed in the town. We needed to turn back. Yes, it was regrettable, but at least we knew Cáceres had a hospital. And it was Sunday, which meant no buses were running and we were informed there was no chance of getting a taxi today, and so we had to walk back.

While packing our gear, we struck up a conversation with the Spanish cyclists. They were drinking coffee and playing hip-hop on a mobile phone. I gave one of them, Ricardo, my Bluetooth speaker. He was delighted. He was also interested that we came from Australia.

'I have always wanted to go to New Zealand,' he said. 'New Zealand has mountains. It is my dream and you are so close in Australia.'

'Do you know much about Australia?' I asked. 'Are you interested in visiting Australia?'

Ricardo smiled sheepishly. 'No, not really.'

I asked the others to pose for a photo on the steps. The two (now cheery) Spaniards cycled off, and surprisingly, Sasha waved us away when we offered to have breakfast and coffee with him. It wasn't quite an abrupt goodbye – rather, he seemed to have found a renewed sense of purpose. He was a man on a mission and there was no time to waste – perhaps his nocturnal texting had helped him find the next clue in his journey. He gave us each a warm hug and strode off.

A short while later we ran into Lea and Dan in the street while we searched for some breakfast. They had stayed in a private *casa rurale* down the road and were heading out of town. It was good to see them. We spoke only briefly, explaining my injury and saying we hoped to catch up with them perhaps in a week.

It took us most of the day to hobble back to Cáceres. I don't remember much of it but I was relieved when I saw the city's outline on the horizon. We found the hotel we had stayed in only two days earlier, the King Alfonso IX, and were glad to hear they had a room available. I studied myself in the mirror and could barely recognise the person looking back; I had lost weight and looked the thinnest I had ever been. What was most concerning was the very noticeable curve in my spine. Cici tried to conceal her alarm. 'Oh boy,' she said. 'We need to go to the hospital.'

At the front desk, the hotel clerk was eager to answer our questions about how to get to the *urgencias* (medical emergency department in the hospital) by public transport, as I doubted I could walk the distance.

'You will need to take a bus.'

'This goes directly to the hospital?'

'Yes, a bus.'

'And where can we find this bus?'

'At the bus stop.'

'And where is that?'

'Where the buses leave from.'

The absurdity of our conversation reminded me of a scene from a Peter Sellers film, and instead of feeling annoyed I started laughing. 'Are you Swiss?' I asked.[6]

He apologised for his limited English and drew a map showing us the bus stop and the hospital. I apologised for my bad Spanish.

In the waiting area of the emergency ward, I reflected on the irony of the situation. For the past three weeks, I'd worried about Cici hurting herself. What if she becomes injured and we can't finish the Camino? What if she has an accident? What if we get hopelessly lost and run out of time? The 'what if' scenarios hadn't taken into account the possibility that I would be the cause of the worry!

---

[6] *In The Revenge of the Pink Panther*, Peter Sellers meets a Swiss innkeeper who has a dog sitting at his feet. He enquires, 'Does your dog bite?' and the innkeeper replies, 'No.' Peter Sellers bends down to pat it and is immediately set upon by the dog as he buries its teeth into his hand. The innkeeper stands by impassively. After fighting off the dog, Sellers says, 'I thought you said your dog did not bite.' The innkeeper replies, 'This is not my dog.'

We sat in the waiting room for most of the afternoon. From time to time, the administration staff poked their heads around the corner, speaking quickly in Spanish. They wanted to see proof of our travel insurance, which we had, but it didn't seem to be what they needed. There were moments when I thought we would be turned out on the street because we couldn't produce the correct document or ID. Eventually, an older doctor came to introduce himself and I hobbled to his office.

'How did you do this?' he asked in English.

'The Camino,' I explained. 'I am doing the Camino.'

He looked at me over the top of his glasses and asked me to lie face down on the bed while he examined my back.

'Please sit down again.' He wrote some notes on his pad.

'I am going to refer you to a special physiotherapist in Cáceres. You will need to see them every day for four days and then we will see…'

'Will I be able to continue?'

'We will see,' he repeated. He handed me a script and signalled that the consultation had ended.

As I started to lift myself unsteadily out of the chair, the doctor asked, 'And what do you normally do for a living?'

I told him.

'So in your line of work do you normally walk 20 or 30 kilometres a day?'

'No, of course not.'

He looked at me again over his glasses. 'So what did you expect?'

For the next four days, I enjoyed sleeping in each morning, which relaxed my mind and body. I visited the physiotherapist for an hour each day. Each visit, the physiotherapist applied electrodes to my back, like clothes pegs, connected to a battery unit, and I felt my back muscles being stimulated. After a few minutes, she increased the power. She repeated this every ten minutes until it became painful, but just before it got too much, she turned the unit off and asked me to return the next day. I think the electrical stimulation reset my muscles, which had been anticipating more pain and torture and so were automatically spasming each time I tried to walk more than ten steps. On my fourth visit to the physiotherapist, there was a noticeable improvement.

Our time of convalescence allowed us to explore this city further. We also celebrated our wedding anniversary. I arranged dinner in a nice restaurant – a luxury – and for dessert Cici took me to a café she had found the day before. She remarked on its beautiful lanterns that hung like chrysalises to illuminate the courtyard; it reminded her of a fairy dell. We sat alone sipping tea and eating delicious chocolate torte.

Later she led me to a tenth-century taverna in the old quarter of the city. It was empty when we arrived except for a cat that sat like an Egyptian statue on the bar. The room had a vaulted ceiling. Candles provided the only light, and the pew-like chairs and altar-like counter made the space feel ecclesiastical. The barman, a cheerful fellow with a Dali-like waxed moustache, appeared and I ordered a Spanish brandy. In that moment, sipping my drink in the quiet, watched over by the sphinx-like cat, I felt truly relaxed for the first time since we had left Seville.

A sign indicating an albergue was always a welcome sight as we entered a town –
in this case, Aljucén.

There were still chores to be done after our 28-kilometre day to Torremejía, where the
albergue (Palacio de los Lastra) was housed in a former monastery.

Rested up and on the road to Casar de Cáceres.

As we entered Mérida, we crossed over the Guadiana River on the Puente Romano, or Roman Bridge, which dates from the first century BC. The world's longest surviving bridge from ancient times, it was once more than 750 metres in length.

In Mérida, we saw storks – it was the first time we had ever seen them except in childhood fairy tales.

Looking down on the plaza
from the Church of San
Francisco Javier, Cáceres.

Our compact monastery cell
in Alcuéscar where Mike's
bed collapsed.

At the Jesuit College in
Villafranca de los Barros, Cici
reconnected with her purpose on
the Camino.

Empathising with our pilgrim
'sole' mate – a statue in Mérida.

Church of San Francisco Javier, Cáceres.

A typically stony path – somewhere on the way to Alcuéscar.

Reconnecting with our compadres Lea and Dan in Cáceres.

Behind the heavy, sometimes fortified, doors is another world hidden from strangers like us.

Streets of the old city in Cáceres – the Camino waits for us in the background.

25-10-2016

Tlf: 923 344 075
e-mail: reservas@turismoruralvilcarreras.es
Calle del Corpus 10 - 12 San Pedro de Rozados
SALAMANCA

Cáceres to Zamora
Chapter 4

26/10/2016

27/10/2016

CALZADA
DE VALDUNCIEL
SALAMANCA

29-10-2016

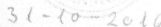

31-10-2016

Blessings in Disguise

Cici

The following morning we prepared to leave Cáceres to travel by bus to Cañaveral, bypassing Casar de Cáceres. We packed up, bid the hotel staff a fond farewell and grabbed some breakfast.

I was in a very reflective mood, casting my mind back on all that had transpired in the past week. I thought of the albergue in Casar de Cáceres, where I had been the only woman among the 14 pilgrims. I had learned to find myself a bottom bunk near a wall and to use my poncho as a screen, tucked into the mattress above, to provide me with some privacy. It was this exact situation, of mixed gender dorms, and bunks in close proximity, that had so confronted me a couple of weeks ago, but now I had surrendered to the environment and found myself adapting. So far, this southern Camino was overwhelmingly made up of male pilgrims. I was becoming acutely aware of being one of the few women walking. Perhaps it was the time of year – late in the walking season.

I thought about our slow return to Cáceres from Casar de Cáceres. Walking along the highway in front of Mike, I had turned around to see how he was doing. I was astonished to see his contorted shape, like a question mark, and the pain in his face that heightened my concern for him. I had felt cranky that we needed to hole up in Caceres again, going nowhere, and wait for our bodies to catch up with our unrealistic expectations of them. It called for a huge psychological adjustment. However, during this second stay we had come to appreciate the city more. It certainly knew us, and we came to know it. We had briefly met another Canadian couple at the hotel, Marilyn and Jack, who were tourists. We introduced them to 'our' Italian restaurant where we shared a meal with them before they moved on to another city.

The next day, mindful of our 17th wedding anniversary, which we had celebrated earlier in the week, Mike bought me a wedding band.

I had been wearing my engagement ring. The owners of the store, a father and son, made the rings themselves. Buying from a family-owned business that had been handed down through the generations felt really special. The owners were proud of their work and were noticeably moved by our purchase in celebration of our special occasion. The son, Manuel, engraved the ring with the words 'For the journey October 2016'. He didn't charge for the extra work. These past few days would be treasured for providing so many rich memories. What had posed a few days earlier as a dismal necessity had turned out to be a true blessing for which we would be forever grateful – Cáceres, our heartfelt thanks.

The bus dropped us in Cañaveral. As we walked down the small main street of the town, we saw a pilgrim standing outside the hostel pulling on her pack ready to start the day. Hiromi was a nurse from Japan and was, at that time, only walking ten kilometres a day while she recovered from her symptoms of bed bug bites from an albergue. She too had been receiving treatment from the emergency department in Cáceres and also taken a bus to Cañaveral. She said she was planning to build up to her regular walking distance in the weeks to come but it was too painful at the moment. We hugged and wished her *Buen Camino*.

We planned to ease back into walking with a shorter day of 14 kilometres and we would be back on track with a longer distance the next day. We arrived in Grimaldo via a winding bush track that followed a steady incline. As we climbed out from the bracken, a bar appeared. Finally! In Spain, a 'bar' is a bar, café and restaurant combined, and a hub where the community can gather as well. It was hot and we were hanging out for our bottles of iced Fanta. It had become our habit to arrive at a café-bar in the middle of the day and order '*Dos Fantas, por favor*'. It was crowded inside the bar so we slumped in chairs out on the small patio, sipping the ice-cold drinks while our core temperatures returned to normal. We weren't able to rest for long, however, as smokers appeared and took over our air space.

We decided to shoulder our packs and look for the albergue, thinking we would come back later to eat. There was nothing to the town except two bars, a large accommodation building down the road that was closed for the season, and an albergue next door to 'Bar Grimaldo'. We were the only pilgrims there, thank goodness – it was tiny. The stone cottage was very modest and consisted of three very small rooms and an entry. The bathroom was so narrow that when I rehearsed sitting on the toilet, which was plumbed facing a sidewall, my knees touched the opposite wall. Later, the bar owner told us that many years ago the albergue had been his family home. His mother had wished for it to be used for the care of pilgrims after her death – for resting weary heads and recovering souls, in return for a small donation.

Having showered and feeling rested, we ate with the locals that night at the bar next door where the barman served a meal he was clearly proud of. Being a vegetarian, I prayed it wouldn't be a plate brimming with *jamón*; if it was, I would need to improvise. There were, however, chips, bread, a side salad, a huge slice of pork (which I passed to Mike), and of course our glass of *vino tinto*. As we ate, the locals watched the football, yelling, roaring with laughter and drinking. All was well and we expressed our appreciation. As there weren't any shops in the town and the bar wouldn't be open when we left in the morning, we asked the owner if he could make us up some food, including a piece of fruit. We also bought large bottles of water.

Arriving back at the albergue we inspected the small entry and living area. Now feeling more settled, I took the time to see what this room offered. A little shrine on one wall depicted Mary and St James, reflecting the intention of the owners to welcome and care for *peregrinos* just like us. There was a small donation box where we could leave a contribution for our night's stay, and hanging on the opposite wall was a framed blessing in Spanish.

Earlier in our journey we had virtually run from towns like this one because there was 'nothing there'. We had wanted to move on to something that felt more familiar, as we were so far out of our comfort zone. I had felt continually isolated by the lack of English conversation, depressed by food I couldn't eat, the intense heat, managing cold sores, cuts, blisters, and grazed shoulders and hips. Grimaldo was similar to some of the other small towns, but it felt different – or was it me who was different? Until now, too often I had allowed the 'not enough' mind-set to take over, thinking there had to be 'something else' or 'more', or 'what will I do now?' The shrine in this albergue sparked something within me. It reminded me why I was walking this path just as visiting the Jesuit college earlier in the walk had touched me. I needed to stop, listen and hear. The framed blessing on the wall, written by Antonio Hernández Martin, resonated deeply for me – it was as though someone knew exactly how I felt and could read my thoughts.

Peregrinos a Santiago

El cansancio en tu cuerpo ya se nota
y tu cuerpo se resiente al caminar
pero no des por admitida tu derrota
sé valiente y esfuérzate en llegar.
Continúa con esa fe de Peregrino
porque esa fe te llevará hasta ese Santo
que te absorbe poco a poco a tu destino
para disfrutar de su imagen y su encanto.
Aunque sufras el cansancio de tus pies
no hagas nunca de pereza ni un amago
porque orgulloso te encontrarás después
cuando estés ante la imagen de Santiago.
Cumplirás lo que habías prometido
y sentirás de ti mismo tal proeza
que aunque llegues a Santiago ya rendido
notarás unos aires de grandeza.
Y quedará en el archivo de tu mente
la hazaña que lograste en su día
que contarás en el entorno de tu gente
y aplaudirán a tu fe y valentía.

written by Antonio Hernández Martin

Pilgrims to Santiago

The tiredness in your body can be seen
and your body feels resentment when walking
but do not give in to defeat
be brave and strive to arrive.
Continue with that Pilgrim faith
because that faith will take you to that Saint
that absorbs you little by little to your destiny
to enjoy of his image and his wonder.
Even though you suffer the tiredness of your feet
do not ever be lazy or feint
because you will find yourself later proud
when you are standing before the image of Santiago.
You will fulfil what you have promised
and you will feel such a feat of yourself
that even though you arrive already worn out
you will notice an air of greatness.
And it will be filed in your mind
the achievement that you reached on your day
that you will recount to your people
and they will applaud your faith and courage.

written by Antonio Hernández Martin

Before we had parted from our American friends in Granada all those weeks ago, Andy had given Mike and me a small scallop shell each to accompany us on our journey. The next morning I left mine on the little shrine in Grimaldo as an offering, along with a blessing I wrote for others. We had both felt cared for in this space.

May the persons caring for the pilgrims
feel richly blessed in life
May the pilgrims who rest here
Find comfort and peace
May the moon and the stars
Shine light on your path
May you see life anew
May all who pass this 'Way'
Feel blessed and revived

– Cici Edwards-Jensen, 2016

We left the town at our usual time of six o'clock in the morning. We decided not to make our way back to the Camino via the bush track at the back of the town, but to try an alternative route further down the highway. It would be a long 33 kilometres to Carcaboso.

About an hour later we were in the middle of nowhere walking single-file along the bitumen highway. As I kept pace with Mike's steady gait, I stopped to take a photo of him on the wide empty road ahead. I was looking down and about to take the photo when I spotted, next to my feet in the long grass, a small wooden cross. I couldn't believe I had stopped at this particular spot. As I picked it up, I noticed it had been carved by hand. So much attention had gone into the making of it that it must have been significant to someone. The cross then stayed in my pocket until the end of our trip. My intention when I found it was to leave it in the cathedral in Santiago, but I took it home with me as a reminder to be grateful for all I am blessed with in my life, and to be present to compassion and love for others in my every day.

We continued to come across many near empty towns with dilapidated homes and I was struck by the brokenness of these places. The economy over the decades had suffered, yet in these abandoned little towns, some people hung on, perhaps with nowhere to move on to. Day by day these villages were exposing more of their decay and vulnerability. I wondered if these crumbling desolate places were asking me to see beyond the physical images of brokenness. Was there something I needed to learn? Was this journey asking me to share my own brokenness as part of who I am? I walked in silence for hours reflecting on my work in pastoral care and the parallels being offered to me. Every day, patients at the hospital shared intimate life stories of their pain, grief and loss, often leaving their hearts exposed, and now I felt I was being asked to do the same.

After 21 kilometres, we arrived in the walled city of Galisteo, stopping for a drink and to have our credentials stamped at the old stone town hall. We spotted a little store that sold the lollies we indulged in around three o'clock each afternoon as a little ritual. I loved the blackberry ones the best. Mike had become the 'lolly keeper' so I wouldn't chew through them too soon. There was a restaurant on the way out of town that was still open so we stopped for lunch.

But getting started again was another story as Mike's back was not up for the next ten kilometres – he couldn't take another step. I asked at the bar if there were any taxis as the bus had already left. The barman rang for one and we waited outside for about 30 minutes as the restaurant was closing up for siesta. The taxi dropped us in Carcaboso outside the albergue Eleni where again we were the only pilgrims. The albergue was a two-storey building facing the main street through town. It had homely touches like patterned tablecloths, family photos on the walls and lots of wooden furniture. We had a comfortable bedroom of our own.

Later that afternoon, walking around town, we saw the mobile home of Marga and Jesús, the Spanish couple we'd first met in El Real de la Jara when we were only a few days into our walking. Marga had walked up to us in a café and asked in a Brooklyn accent whether we were walking the Vía de la Plata. Her parents had moved to New York when she was a child then returned to Spain when she was in her twenties. Walking the Camino appeared to be more Jesús's calling than hers. Marga struggled with the heat but still wanted to accompany him. She carried a sun umbrella and smoked cigarettes, and Jesús carried a small daypack and a huge camera, taking many photos along the path. In Spanish, Jesús is pronounced 'hey Zeus'. When Marga first introduced Jesus, we thought she'd said Hortense, or maybe Horace. Mike, confused, was using both names, and Jesús kept correcting him by saying 'hey Zeus', but we didn't realise this until later.

We were so happy to see them again. We were invited into their little mobile home, along with their beagle Breza, and Jesús offered us his homemade liquor and Belgian chocolates. He showed us photos of flocks of birds and flowers that had caught his eye on the trail. Marga asked how we were going to manage the next leg – it was 41 kilometres to Aldeanueva del Camino.

'I know,' I said. 'I've been studying the guidebook. I know we can't make it further than the Arch of Cáparra because of Mike's back.'

Marga said something to Jesús and he made a call to a hotel on the highway not far from the Camino. The hotel offered a service for a fee where someone would collect pilgrims in a car, take them to the hotel for the night and drop them back again the next day.

Marga translated what Jesús was saying: 'Oh hello. Is that the Hotel Asturias? I have two pilgrims from Australia, a married couple. Yes, they have come from Australia! The wife is very beautiful and the husband unfortunately is not so much. Could you please arrange to pick them up from the Arch...?'

Marga and Jesús were ending their Camino that day because Marga's mother had become ill. They invited us to have a meal at their home in Santiago de Compostela when we arrived later the following month. We were very grateful to them for arranging the lift.

As arranged, the driver came to collect us at the agreed place and time and we stayed a night at the hotel, which was located in a very remote spot. The next morning, the driver dropped us back at the Arch to walk to Aldeanueva del Camino and then on to Baños de Montemayor.

Baños de Montemayor is renowned for its thermal springs and spas, and by the time we arrived, three weeks into our Camino, we had walked 34 kilometres that day and had reached the 450-kilometre mark. For the first time, I was aware of how much closer we were to Santiago, and it felt as though we had come a great distance. I was pleased, but with still so far to go, I didn't want to take a chance of going 'soft' on myself so I didn't book in for a soak in the spa. I was afraid to relax in case it made me realise just how tired and sore I really was. I also thought it would make it difficult to start out uphill the next day. We found the albergue, which turned out to be the best on the whole of the Camino, had a good sleep, and were provided with a prepared continental breakfast the next morning – this was simply unheard of until now.

We began the hike out of town with a one-hour ascent and 570 kilometres still ahead of us. As we walked, I looked back and my eyes followed the mist-laden valley that led to the bluest of reservoirs in the far distance. The hills on either side seemed to cup the water between their strong and nurturing flanks. We headed into the mountains leaving the Castile Region behind and entered the province of Salamanca where we expected cold and rainy weather.

After an easy morning walk, we arrived in the very old and small village of Calzada de Béjar. Not far away, up in the mountains, was the medieval city of Béjar, which was off the Camino and on our agenda. The city had a long and rich religious history which we were excited to explore, however, our schedule didn't allow us to walk there so we decided to speak to locals to find some transport. Manuela, the lady who ran the albergue, Alba y Soraya, in Calzada de Béjar, graciously gave permission for us to take her photo. She stamped our credentials and directed us to the only bar in town where we grabbed a coffee and found a local who drove the only taxi.

The taxi wound its way up the mountain, around and around, and as we reached the peak, Béjar appeared in a massive valley below us. We took in the astounding view of the city, and descended towards it, weaving our way down, driving parallel to the ancient stone walls. We made arrangements with the taxi driver to pick us up from the same spot at six o'clock the following morning, and bid him *adios*. He was more than pleased to accommodate us, as the fare was a substantial amount for him, but it wasn't so much to us.

We found a 1970s hotel about half a kilometre away to stay the night. We ventured out to find a pharmacy where we could buy a support bandage as my ankle had begun to click out of place (I was waiting to see what might crack and fall off next!).

We began to explore this extraordinary city, which was founded in 400 BC. Over the centuries, different communities have added their story to its many layers. Without a guide or a guidebook we wandered the streets and lanes taking in the styles of buildings from different eras. The old Jewish quarter, which had once thrived, was now marked with plaques telling a story of the trades and the communities that had occupied these streets and lanes centuries ago. Lanes opened up to squares, and one square opened up to a wide flight of steps that led to a grand manor house, which had once belonged to a powerful family. Mike took my photo while I sat on a bench between stunning statues of Don Quixote and Sancho Panza.

Climbing along the top of the old wall that encircled Béjar, we marvelled at the view across the valley as the sun set. Feeling hungry and tired we set off in search of dinner. Despite Béjar's size, we couldn't find a café or restaurant open (or shut for that matter). It took us until nearly nine o'clock to find a hotel with a dining room where we could order tapas and wine (the barman said it was still too early to order dinner).

When we returned to our hotel, the large reception area looked permanently closed. We saw no signs of other guests. The rooms were tidy but looked frozen in a bygone era – brown, dimly lit, and featuring brown and gold striped bed covers and cushions. The hotel was a bit like the town – a relic of more prosperous times when once Béjar buzzed with cafés and restaurants filled with locals and tourists.

The next morning we were up and out in the dark to meet the taxi as planned to drive us back to Calzada de Béjar. We resumed the Camino where we had left off the day before, but within half an hour we knew we were off course in a remote area of farmland. We had stopped to check our guidebook in the driveway of a farm when by sheer good fortune we met the farmer, who offered to drive us two kilometres in his truck to have us back on track. We were amazed to learn that this man, Juan Maxi, was the husband of Manuela whom we had met the day before at the albergue. What a stroke of luck! I notched this up as another example of being 'cared for'. I gave the farmer my new scarf, which I had bought in Cáceres, to give to Manuela as an offering of gratitude. Once again, we had connected with very kind and caring people.

Now heading on the correct path, we began to relax into the morning and to be more present to our day. We experienced a glorious sunrise with rays streaming through the clouds and radiating soft light upon the fields. A perfect semicircle of a rainbow, vividly coloured, appeared so close and yet so far away. It was a beautiful morning in many ways, but unfortunately by the time we reached Fuenterroble de Salvatierra I was struggling with the combination of heat and radiating nerve pain, which was almost unbearable.

As we walked into town, we saw small whitewashed stone buildings on either side of the main street. Fuenterroble resembled a town in an old cowboy movie, complete with the odd tumbleweed. Towards the end of town we came across the albergue, and what a welcome sight it was. As we stood in the shade of the grapevine-covered entry, volunteers came out to greet us, led us inside and took our packs. Their welcome was so warm and friendly.

In our experience, meeting people on the Camino was often like running into old friends you haven't seen for some time. That may sound strange but it is exactly how I always felt. A little kindness goes a long way and it is never taken for granted or forgotten. One of the volunteers who greeted us was Gretel from Holland, who spoke English and was wonderfully supportive. We also met Antonio, Inyucki the cook, and a Swiss couple, Cornelia (Connie) and Andreas, who also spoke English. I felt happy to be connected and for a little while to experience a feeling of communion. We were offered a modest lunch of soup, bread and fruit which hit the spot.

Gretel offered to take me in a cab to the hospital to have my pain addressed. I thought, *Here we go again!* This had become a familiar experience. We chatted along the way about so many things, feeling as though we had known each other for ages, and I forgot the discomfort of my leg for the duration of the ride. As usual, the medical staff shook their heads in disbelief at how far we had come (the flight from Australia and the walk from Seville) and what we were trying to accomplish. They were very attentive and caring.

Back at the albergue I found a bunk to call my own. As I unpacked, I noticed the communal bathroom empty of other pilgrims. I enjoyed a relaxing hot shower and took the opportunity to rest for a couple of hours on my bunk in the quiet.

Later, the priest, Don Blas, and Inyucki the cook showed us around and spoke of the wonderful work being done to help people in the area. There were three prongs to Don Blas's work: the albergue to support the pilgrims; a children's school, which he initiated and where he teaches as part of his ministry for the marginalised; and his working farm of donkeys. When he finds the time, Don Blas also leads pilgrimages of approximately 250 people, with his donkeys and a wooden cart, across France to Italy. We sat around the table as a family, full of gratitude for each other, and shared a hearty evening meal. During the night I heard Mike get up to gather firewood to feed the fire in the potbelly stove in the corner of the room so everyone could sleep warmly. I felt I had been whining with my injury, yet I was reminded constantly of all I was thankful for, including Mike's gift of warmth.

The next day we rode the bus to Salamanca, where I would rest my leg, and Mike, his back. Writing this I am having a laugh – what a couple of broken beings we had become. Two days later, we left our packs at the hotel and caught a taxi back to where we had left the Camino so we could make up for the kilometres we had 'lost' by taking the bus. The taxi driver was quite perplexed when we asked him to drop us in the middle of nowhere, but we reassured him we would be fine. I felt carefree with only our small daypacks. Once we had covered the kilometres we needed to do, we caught a bus the rest of the way back to Salamanca. As we walked around the Plaza Mayor late in the afternoon, we heard a familiar voice.

'It's the Australians!' We turned to see our fellow pilgrims, Lea and Dan. I was so excited to see them! In a great stroke of timing, they were on the end of a couple of rest days. It was hugs all round.

We repeated the same process the following day, hailing a taxi, driving 24 kilometres out, and then walking back into the city across the famous Roman bridge, having made up our kilometres. Walking without a full pack was working well for me.

On our final day of rest, Mike and I explored Salamanca separately, allowing each other some space. Given we had been spending 24 hours a day, seven days a week together under difficult circumstances, we were doing well travelling in each other's pockets. A month earlier, reading the online Camino Forum, I had come across a post from a woman who was walking the Camino Francés with her partner, asking, 'What decision should I make?' She was pondering whether to stay with him and carry on bickering, or just leave him. I had laughed out loud and wondered if it could happen to us.

Whenever I found I was 'in a mood' or in pain or just too tired to cope, I would let Mike know that I wasn't going to talk for the remainder of the day. He probably thought, *I can be so lucky!* It was the only way I could keep some perspective and not say – out of pure frustration – something I might later regret. I relieved my frustration by going to 'pity land' and having a cry, whereas at home I would have headed out to a café, to 'latte land', so this was the next best thing. Anyway, it worked for me and for Mike. When we were both quiet for hours on end, it was actually a blessing in disguise. After all my inner ranting had settled and silence had risen to the top, I could once again be present to my inner domain and listen to what was happening for me. Slowly, a more peaceful and less begrudging space opened up; my body softened and I felt kinder to myself instead of beating myself up for not coming up to par. If I needed to walk slower, or felt another physical symptom, or felt too tired to carry on, I thought of myself as failing. The heaviest pressure I felt was coming from myself. I have been well trained in this. I realise I have always felt this from my childhood. Being the eldest of five I felt the weight of duty and responsibility at a young age to care for my siblings before myself. Mum was often unwell and sometimes hospitalised which meant I missed long periods of schooling to help out at home. (Especially early in my high school years when Dad needed to work seven days a week.) From the age of 10, I was bringing in the washing, sorting and ironing, preparing meals, changing nappies and placating a baby on my hip. For my escape, I would ride my bike the couple of kilometres down to the sea finding a bench near the foreshore under the strong and nurturing canopy of a Moreton Bay Fig tree. I would sometimes be accompanied by my little transistor radio – other times I just needed to close my eyes and listen to the gentle rhythmic roll of the loyal waves rocking my soul.

On my day alone, I went to Mass at the majestic cathedral, had my credentials stamped, and looked in the shops for a couple of souvenirs. I was thinking of home because one of my best friends, Robyn, was turning 60 without me. I later borrowed Mike's phone to order and send her red roses. She was foregoing having a big party for this milestone because I wasn't going to be there with her. Forty-one years of true friendship.

Mike and I met up for a late lunch and a stroll in the cathedral garden, which was nestled in a secluded spot behind the cathedral. We walked through an entry in the old stone wall and were treated to an oasis. Straight ahead, in the centre of the garden, stood an ancient well covered by a leafy arch, which in turn was sheltered from the sun by tall trees planted at intervals in the stone paving. There were few other people, and standing there, shaded by the cool leaves and touched by the quiet, gave a sense of being in a sacred space and/or a secret garden. I remember smiling and feeling so relaxed as we ambled to the far side of the garden to enjoy the view across the city.

As much as it had been nice to rest up, I felt the urge to be back on the track. We had now walked 511 kilometres; there were 483 to go. The heat had barely eased, and the temperature was still 25 degrees Celsius at ten o'clock that night.

October had come to an end. Having walked for a month, we arrived at El Cubo, another small town with the usual whitewashed stone cottages. This one, however, was reasonably well populated and had two bars spilling over with patrons. It was great to see everyone out and about; normally the streets were deserted when we arrived during siesta. We appeared to be a point of interest as we made our way down the main street.

The first bar we stopped at was brimming with lads in full voice. We found a table at the second bar and ordered our usual couple of cold Fantas. I rarely drink soft drink at home, but we really looked forward to it when we reached a town after a day of walking in the heat. The Fanta was cold, tangy and fizzy, and hit the spot on a hot dry throat (sounding like a beer commercial I know). There were some seafood tapas on the bar, so we ordered a couple each, and bought some bottles of water for the next day.

It was time to throw our packs on again and look for an albergue. We found a privately owned one run by Carmen, her adult daughter Mercedes, and her son-in-law Fernando. Carmen had set up the albergue wishing to care for and support pilgrims on their journey. We had a shower and hand-washed some clothes. Mercedes showed us around the town, which was really kind. She said there was not a lot to eat in the town in the way of a nutritious meal, and offered to cook for us that night in the home she shared with Carmen, Fernando and their two small children. The family didn't normally eat dinner until much later in the evening, so they were quite amused that we wanted to eat at seven.

Mike and I sat at a table with the family looking on and we covered our legs with a large shared blanket. After a while, I began to feel very hot. I lifted the blanket under the tablecloth to see a briquette fire burning away in a metal container – effective, for sure. We were served tortilla, soup, cod, and a sweet flan, which we know as crème caramel. I couldn't possibly eat it all and was very apologetic.

Mercedes spoke English quite well, and she told us about being a woman in her culture, and about the hardship in her village brought on by the downturn in the economy. Fernando had a work injury and had no money coming in, so

Mercedes worked a few jobs to make ends meet. We said goodnight at about 9.30 pm, explaining we needed to be up very early. The little ones were still watching cartoons on the TV. Mercedes and Fernando offered to make us up some food for our journey the next day.

That night in bed, I noticed that the little blankets were handmade and had been finished with blanket stitch, which I hadn't seen for many years. I was transported to a time in my childhood when the blanket on my bed was finished in the same way. This lovely touch of simplicity and homeliness should have given me a sense of comfort and safety, but I remembered, as a child, pulling the blanket up over my head with my pillow on top to muffle the yelling from my father and the screams from my mother.

At that moment in time, so far from home, this memory felt a lifetime ago and incongruent with the love, care and kindness I had experienced on the Camino. In my work, and in the media, it is not uncommon to hear people say of their abusers, 'he/she doesn't mean it. I love him/her and she/he loves me. It will work out. It will be okay.' When I was growing up, it was not uncommon for children to receive regular beltings at the hands of 'loving' and very sad, powerless or angry parents. My family wasn't any different. I grew up thinking all families treated each other in this way, and nobody ever spoke of it outside the home.

Fernando was up early the next morning to offer us a small breakfast and we asked him to stamp our credentials. We paid for the night's accommodation and food and offered something extra for our hosts' kindness. We were very thankful for their hospitality and thoughtfulness. This stay would be one of our cherished memories.

Mike

Having climbed steadily out of the dry brown plains in the past few days, we were now into the mountains. We saw more small (partly) abandoned villages where a few residents had somehow hung onto their land holdings and nurtured small vegetable patches. There was no attempt to fix or repair what had broken. Cici found these villages deeply moving – that people could somehow accept such brokenness in their lives and even find meaning in it. 'It's because they had no money to repair it,' I said. Cici frowned. Had I missed the point or not seen her perspective on things again?

Walking through the steep mountains took its toll on Cici, whereas I had always enjoyed walking uphill more than trudging across the flats. When I walk up any incline, whether it's a mountain or a hill or even a long flight of stairs, I feel energised and often become talkative.

Cici, in contrast, tended to stop talking as she grew weary of the incline. I hadn't realised she was experiencing a lot of nerve pain.

'Cici, I was thinking when we get back home, we could get some electric gates to replace those old wooden ones. You know how they're such a pain in winter – we hate them, right? Imagine how much better it would be! You wouldn't even have to get out of the car. Whaddaya think?'

No response.

Ten minutes went by.

I tried to think of something encouraging and inspiring to say.

'We could even get some faux wood gates! That would look good, don't ya think?'

Towards nightfall we walked into Baños de Montemayor, where traditionally the wealthy came to 'take the waters'. Baños's main street was filled with old buildings that had once been grand hotels. Some of them still were. The old lamps threw out a yellow hue that reminded me of romantic images of old English country towns. We climbed up through the steep streets – typically, the last few hundred metres of the day were the hardest when our reserves of energy and patience were almost empty.

The albergue was located at the highest point in town, but it was worth the climb: modern, inviting and amazingly, almost empty. There was only one other pilgrim, an Italian named Pietro who was, I guessed, in his late sixties. A large, strong-looking man with a grey beard and soft, perhaps sad, features, he was walking the Camino on his own. We had the pick of the beds – and yes, there were beds with sheets. There were even desktop Apple Macs for pilgrims to use, and free printing! The standard of albergues was so variable. It was one of the surprises that kept us guessing before we arrived at each destination – what would the albergue be like? The high level of comfort in Baños reflected the wealth of the town, in contrast to the more economically depressed villages we had stayed in so far.

Later, towards dinnertime, we wandered back through the same lanes, which were even harder to manage going downhill without slipping on the cobblestones. I marvelled at the way older folk here seemed to climb the lanes with only minimal support from their walking sticks. We arrived at a restaurant and discovered our Italian friend had already found it.

Pietro was not fluent in English but we managed to learn about him and his life as we ate pizza and shared a bottle of red. There was gentleness about him, a soft way of speaking that perhaps made us warm to him. He was from northern Italy, which, like Spain, has been gutted by the global financial crisis since 2008. After his engineering business went broke, his wife died of cancer. I don't know if he had any children – he didn't speak of any. He had not been back home much. He said he had walked out his front door one day and had just kept walking, becoming, it seemed, a life pilgrim, walking many of the different Caminos in Europe.

We shared a simple meal. There was no conversation in the conventional sense: we didn't share our views or information about our families, and I didn't know what he liked or what he thought. But for me, the experience transcended the superficiality of our words and the limitations of not having a shared language. I felt a deep connection with him. Maybe this was the beginning of the 'spiritual' creeping into my experience of the Camino. Our time together felt special, if not sacred. Back at the albergue, when we said goodnight to Pietro and wished each other well, it was as if I were saying, 'Travel well in your life, dear friend! May you be watched over!'

In the morning, I enjoyed the view from the shower, which had a window that overlooked the valley and farmlets. But it didn't occur to us to linger in this beautiful town because we felt we had to make up for lost time after our delay in Cáceres. When I stepped into the street, I felt the bracing air of the higher altitude. It was already eight o'clock. The sun was nowhere in sight, not like in the south, where by now its ruddy colours would be smeared across the sky as it climbed onto its throne looking angry and red. We pushed on into the mountains thinking, *The worst of it is over.*

I had looked forward to arriving in the city of Salamanca for many weeks. The city represented a significant psychological milestone being the halfway point in our journey. When we finally walked in, I snapped a photo of Cici on the Roman arched bridge that led to the gates of the city. I could hardly believe it – we had walked 570 kilometres.

For the past ten days, I have been engrossed in reading about Spanish history and the civil war[7] in particular. I learned it was a time when the rest of Europe and the world stood back and watched as Russia and the Fascist powers meddled in the internal battle between Franco's forces and the Republicans. Nobody in the international community came to Spain's aid. In the end, what little help did come was from individuals around the world. Motivated by courage and idealism, an international brigade of individual volunteers walked away from their normal lives to come to Spain and fight Franco's nationalist forces, who were supported by arms and armies from fascist Germany and Italy. I was astonished that individuals felt roused to do this, and so soon after the Great War. They came from Canada, Australia, the USA and the UK, and they included writers and journalists such as Laurie Lee, Ernest Hemingway and Martha Gellhorn. I read their books as a teenager, but I had been oblivious to the historical context of their writing.

Reading about the Spanish Civil War affected me more than I expected. It reconnected me with images I have known all my life, such as the famous shot by the Hungarian wartime photographer Robert Capa. It shows a young soldier as he leaps from his trench and is hit by a bullet. Another is the picture of a mother and small child running through the streets of Madrid as they hear the sounds of the bomber planes overhead. You can see the fear in their eyes. I looked at that photo in a bookshop in Salamanca and thought, whatever happened to that little girl? She could still be alive today.

Another reason I had looked forward to Salamanca (apart from the psychological milestone) was that it houses the country's national archives of that war. Salamanca's Civil War Archive holds photos, the newspapers of the day, propaganda posters, relics of everyday life before and during the war, and records of the tens of thousands of people – soldiers and civilians – who remain 'missing'. I was quiet and sombre when I left the building after my visit and emerged into the bright sunshine.

Salamanca itself is a delight for visitors, famous for its Gothic cathedral, its university, its libraries dating back to the 1200s, and a huge beautiful main plaza where people come to sip coffee, drink and meet friends. Cici and I tried our hand at being tourists, wandering through the market squares and streets taking

---

[7] 17 July 1936–1 April 1939.

photos. Shopping for toothpaste and hand-wash, I learned more Spanish phrases, such as *'sin bolsa, por favor'* ('no bag, please') in keeping with our environmental objection to plastic. We rediscovered our favourite Italian restaurant chain, La Tagliatella.

I just wish I could have enjoyed the city more. I had difficulty reconciling its modern, trendy bars and restaurants with the impoverished rural Spain we had experienced. I found it hard to reconcile the loveliness of the present surroundings with the horrors of the past. I had had a similar experience visiting Vietnam a few years ago. I became engrossed in learning about the 'American War' and visiting the museums where the horrors of torture were graphically exhibited. I was left conflicted and unable to participate in, let alone enjoy, being a tourist in Hanoi. Here in Salamanca I felt the same. I watched tourists listening to pre-recorded narratives through headphones on the motorised trains that chug around the city. They all had cameras and seemed to spend most of the tour with their eyes on their cameras' viewfinders. No doubt this was a blessing for people who physically struggled to walk the streets, but I could not imagine doing this myself. I was disdainful and referred to it as the tourists' 'Disneyland' experience. The trauma I had read about, and my visit to the archives, had depressed me and put me in a judgmental frame of mind.

As we walked through the Plaza Mayor, we heard a familiar voice. 'It's the Australians!'

Dan and Lea were sitting at a table sipping wine in the sunshine. They were a picture of relaxed elegance – Lea was wearing a skirt and blouse and Dan wore his Panama hat. We, on the other hand, still wore our tired Camino clothes. How did they manage to achieve such a transformation, from *peregrinos* to urbane tourists? It was good to see them and for a moment I felt lifted out of my melancholic fog. That night we shared dinner in a restaurant not far from the cathedral: wonderful tapas and a main dish of trout poached in milk and herbs. It felt like a world away from the basic meals we had eaten in the small towns and villages. We talked about our respective families in Saskatoon and Melbourne, about our children (and their partners) and the challenges they were going through, which are shared by young adults everywhere – establishing careers, buying a home, and finding their feet in the world. I googled Saskatoon and was surprised by how much its skyline resembled Melbourne's. When I asked Lea if Saskatoon had mountains like other parts of Canada, she and Dan shook their heads.

'It's flat. Just like much of the Meseta we have been walking through.'

'But that will soon change,' Cici reminded us. 'We're getting close to Galicia, and that means mountains. And rain [which she looked forward to].'

It was a wonderful night. The pleasures of good food and good company lightened my mood. By the time dessert arrived, my thoughts of human suffering and the Spanish Civil War had drifted away.

Taking in the expanse of the countryside somewhere between Grimaldo and Galisteo.

The view back to the Ambroz valley and reservoir as we left Baños de Montemayor.

Cici connecting with characters from childhood stories, Don Quixote and Sancho Panza.

The scenery changed as we left Baños de Montemayor behind us and entered the province of Salamanca.

A stony path on a steady incline leading out of Baños de Montemayor.

Homely touches in the albergue Eleni in Carcaboso.

Historic Béjar sits nestled in this beautiful valley where we watched the sunset.

Mike in front of the F & M Albergue in El Cubo, where we had dinner with Mercedes and her family.

Ancient village homes in Calzada de Béjar.

As we left El Cubo, we walked past the church, where Cici was attracted to the morning light and the colour of the wildflowers around the base of the cross.

View from the cathedral gardens, Salamanca.

Saying goodbye to pilgrims and
volunteers at the albergue in
Fuenterroble de Salvatierra.

Meeting and connecting with
Hiromi, a peregrino from Japan.

Our sleeping quarters in the small
albergue in Grimaldo.

Enjoying the vivid colours of this beautiful rainbow one morning on the way to Fuenterroble.

Apart from the dormitory, Don Blas offered alternative accommodation including this stone cottage with a tree growing through the roof.

This design is outside the Bejar Jewish museum. Legend says it symbolises the keys to the houses that the Sephardic jews took with them into exile in hope that they would be able to return to their homes one day. The key is depicted as the tree of life. The dove represents hope.

Baños de Montemayor – 569 kilometres to go until we reach our destination.

Manuela, owner of the albergue in Calzada de Béjar.

The historic Jewish quarter in Béjar.

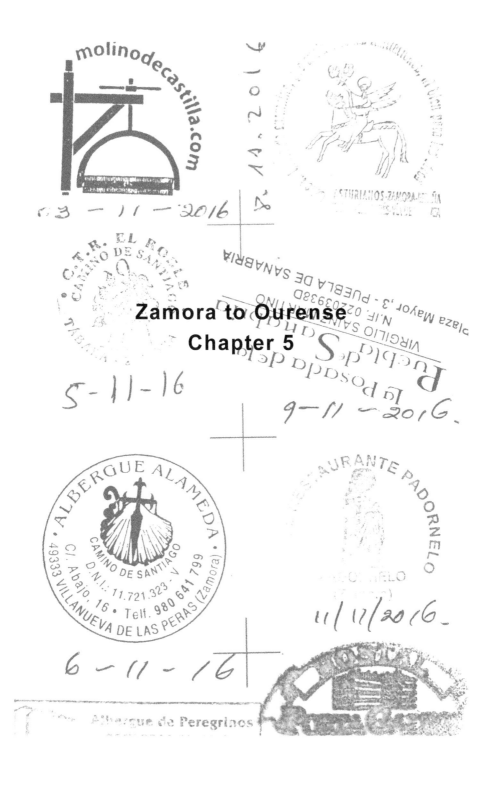

Zamora to Ourense
Chapter 5

molinodecastilla.com

03 — 11 — 2016

8 . 11 . 2016

ASTURIANOS-ZAMORA

C.T.R. EL ROBLE
CAMINO DE SANTIAGO
TABARA

5 - 11 - 16

Puebla de Sanabria
La Posada de...
VIRGILIO SANTIAGO
N.I.F. 02Z03938D
Plaza Mayor, 3 - PUEBLA DE SANABRIA

9 - 11 - 2016

ALBERGUE ALAMEDA
CAMINO DE SANTIAGO
D.N.I.: 11.721.323 - V
C/. Abajo, 16 • Telf. 980 641 799
49333 VILLANUEVA DE LAS PERAS (Zamora)

RESTAURANTE PADORNELO
PADORNELO

11/11/2016

6 — 11 — 16

Albergue de Peregrinos

Tu Camino

Cici

Bonds between pilgrims run strong and deep, so when we reached Zamora, we were shocked and saddened to receive news from Dan and Lea, who were a couple of days in front of us. They had decided to abort their Camino and fly home to Canada. Dan's sister had become very ill and been transferred into palliative care, and Dan himself had fallen ill with a fever and stomach problems. We offered to travel to the town where they were staying and support them as best we could, but they declined. As grateful as they were for our offer, they were managing.

We would stay in Zamora for three nights, glad for the opportunity to experience the comfort of a nice hotel, wash some clothes, and find a physio to treat my right leg. My left leg seemed to be okay now but I had been experiencing pain in my right thigh – in fact, the pain had prompted us to catch a taxi for the last eight kilometres. We would make up the kilometres later, backtracking without our packs.

After settling into a hotel, I went straight to the hairdresser across the road. My Spanish had improved now so I was able to make an appointment and explain what I wanted – I was very proud of myself. Later in the afternoon, after attending the physio, we received a video call on Mike's phone. It was wonderful to see and hear my son Jamieson and his partner Sonya. Before we left home, we had told everyone we wouldn't be available to speak while we were away, but we would email a brief summary of our progress each time we reached a large city. We didn't want to post on Facebook or keep a blog; I would have found social media a constant invasion of my space. I would have had no hope of going within, or just being on my pilgrimage. But this call was so welcome.

After the call, I thought about how much I enjoyed being loved by my family and friends, and how much I loved loving them. It hadn't dawned on me until now how much I missed that connection, which I had deprived myself of over the many weeks on the Camino. So now, two-thirds of the way into the journey, I was confused about how I wanted to continue with the pilgrimage. Before I left home, I believed that to walk my true Camino – to walk it authentically – I had to divorce myself from civilisation and all things familiar. I think this is why I felt torn when I arrived in the cities. I looked forward to entering a city to rest and explore its history but I felt another part of me belonged elsewhere. Ambling through the streets, I would pass a laneway opening on to fields or hills in the distance and it was as though the Camino was waiting there, beckoning my soul. Sometimes I found myself smiling and other times I felt pressured or daunted. But always I was reminded that as much as I may involve or distract myself with the familiar on rest days, this journey was a calling.

Over the next couple of days, using Zamora as our base, we pressed on to the next town, Montamarta, then La Granja, and returned to the city by bus after each day of walking. During one of our day walks, we stopped for lunch amidst the ruins of an abbey that had once been the headquarters of the Knights of Santiago. From the twelfth to the sixteenth century, these warrior monks protected pilgrims en route to Santiago from robbers and Moorish knights. Sitting in this ancient place, deep in thought, I tried to imagine the walls intact, the abbey bustling with people, their life's mission to protect pilgrims. I didn't want to think too much about those who would have been slain. As we were leaving, we met Brien from California, who was walking on his own. We would see more of him in the coming weeks.

The next day, we received another email from Lea to say Dan was feeling a little better. The doctors believed he had a stomach infection from eating undercooked eggs. Further news was that Dan's sister had died while they were in Astorga. They were flying back to Canada the following day to be home in time to attend her funeral. Our dear friends were grieving. They promised they would stay in touch after their return home. Our hearts went out to them – they hadn't been able to return in time to say goodbye to the one they loved. It all seemed to have happened so quickly. It was with heavy hearts we walked that day. Dan and Lea's experience reminded us of our friend Shirley, how we missed her and had not been able to say goodbye or attend her funeral. Her family had been very gracious in asking me to email my thoughts to be read at the funeral, for which I was very grateful. My family had attended the funeral in our place.

The weather had begun to change so in Zamora Mike bought a lightweight coat to replace one he had given away earlier to lighten his load. I bought gloves and a buff (a tubular scarf). We needed our weatherproof ponchos too by the time we reached the next town, Tábara, where we would stay the night. The albergue had been recommended; however when we finally found it on the outskirts of the town, we didn't get a good vibe about staying there and instead, found a room above a pub that offered meals as part of the deal.

Leaving our packs in the room, we diverted off the Camino to a small town, Faramontanos (with a population of only 365 people) to make up some more kilometres. We didn't come across one soul along the road. The only sounds were the pitter-patter of raindrops on our ponchos, the whoosh of the water-spray as the trucks passed, and a flock of playful birds dipping and swooping their way through the rain.

As we approached the town it was distressing to see more forlorn faces of neglected dogs. They were wary of us, standing like statues with their eyes glued to our every move. It was around siesta time and there was no one to be seen. Being curious, we strolled through the cold, wet, narrow streets, interested to see how people lived and what the town might offer.

The rain became heavier and so we sheltered in the only taverna until it eased. The interior was dark and empty except for the bartender and a customer watching the television above the bar. As we began our walk back to Tábara the rain stopped, leaving us to breathe in the freshness and stillness of the late afternoon. There was a soft gentle light peeking through the low-hanging clouds as the sun began to set behind them. I will always remember feeling peaceful and contented that afternoon as we strolled along the edge of the highway past the farms, back into town. That night, it was so good to settle into a warm bed. The noise from the downstairs bar dissolved as sleep quickly overcame me.

The following day we walked into Villaneuva de las Peras having seen no other pilgrims all day, which was becoming the norm. Most of the small town was boarded up. There were two bars, one of which had accommodation, but there were many riders from a motorcycle club in town on a road trip and the rooms were booked out. We were disappointed: it was so cold outside and the hotel restaurant, El Mona, was warm and welcoming. The manager said there was an albergue, but it was closed for the winter. Despite this, he agreed to open it and let us stay for the night. He jumped on his bicycle and we followed him down a few streets to the building. Inside it was freezing. He showed us how to use the heater, which was fuelled by recycled wood pellets that resembled dried cat food.

After a hot shower, we walked back to El Mona for a meal. The manager, Miguel, was very proud of their specialities, although I could only eat sparingly because most of them contained pork. Mike ate enthusiastically. Miguel and his wife were lovely people and thoughtful, caring hosts. We enjoyed their warm restaurant and wonderful hospitality. Later, back at the albergue, it was too cold to sleep in the bedrooms so we closed up the room where the heater rumbled away and slept on the lounge chairs with blankets borrowed from many bunks. Mike was up every couple of hours to feed the cat-pellets to the heater to keep us warm.

Leaving Villaneuva de las Peras in the morning, we passed homes cut into the hillsides with no roofs to be seen (not as we know them anyway) and a thick, deep coverage of grass; the occasional chimney emerged through the grass. We marvelled at their ingenuity and the ecological benefits as well.

Rionegro del Puente was 27 kilometres down the track. It was cold and raining, but we were fortunate to come across a place to eat along the way. We finally arrived around eight o'clock, having walked the last kilometres along the edge of the highway in the dark with our head torches to alert oncoming traffic. I walked in front wearing my bright lime-green poncho that doubled as a beacon in the night.

It was great to find our American friend Brien in the bar when we arrived. Brien is a very trim and fit granddad in his sixties; he writes a travel blog called 'Grandpa's Gone Again'. He is a modest former elite athlete and ultra-marathoner. We were impressed with his accomplishments in life and enjoyed meeting up with him whenever our paths crossed. He had walked the Camino Francés in its entirety with another person, but it hadn't gone so well. He realised afterwards that as an introvert he enjoyed his own company, happy to walk the kilometres listening to his playlist on his iPod.

Brien had eaten earlier and recommended the restaurant over the road. Like many restaurants, it offered pilgrims the *menú del día* (menu of the day). The waiter brought us soup that had lumps of fatty pork floating in it. Mike looked at me, knowing I wouldn't be able to eat it, but I didn't want to offend the friendly waiter. He suggested, when the waiter had returned to the kitchen, that I pour some of it into my coffee mug, take it into the toilet, flush it and race back so it would appear I had been eating. I was mortified at the thought of being caught in this deception, but it was funny at the same time. I made two trips to the toilet and Mike helped out once as well. He also ate all of his own soup. The waiter asked whether I would like some more, but I graciously declined: 'Mmm, but I wouldn't be able to eat the next course.'

Brien, Mike and I were the only occupants in the municipal albergue that night, and it was very nice: modern, clean and – most importantly – warm. We sat in the bunkroom and talked about the people we had met on the Camino. Brien was interested in the idea of '*tu Camino*' (your Camino), meaning there is no 'one way' to do it.

'We can get caught up in doing the Camino a certain way, when in fact some choose to take the bus, ride a bike or only walk the last 100 kilometres,' he said. 'Whatever way you do it, if you do it wholeheartedly, it is true for you.'

This made me think of Kieran, Marga and Jesús, and how their way of walking was different and unique to them. Everyone has their own way of doing things and getting through it. A lot like life, I suppose.

The next morning we said goodbye to Brien and then started on our way to Asturianos – another long day. We didn't take the same path as Brien that morning because of the weather. There had been heavy rains. Brien was prepared to take a chance on the Camino not being flooded. We didn't and so decided to stick to the highway. On arrival, we found the albergue was annexed to a bar that backed onto a gym. There were six bunks in a very small room to bed four people, including Brien and a Spanish pilgrim, Fernando. The heating was extremely poor, especially when Fernando decided to place his wet socks across the only heater. What could we say? He needed dry socks.

The last two long days of walking had affected my left leg again, especially my ankle. Sleep was hard to come by and the showers were in a cavernous, freezing toilet block off the gym. We made do with a good wash as the weather was becoming bitterly cold and the rain was constant. The next morning, it was bliss to find my shoes dry, or mostly dry.

Leaving Asturianos, we walked along a ridge with views into a deep valley and then began our descent, arriving on the outskirts of Puebla de Sanabria. We came across a roadside hotel where we stopped for a small snack as we were unsure how long it would be before we found anywhere else to eat. The hotel was straight out of one of those old American movies, complete with neon signs, semitrailers and giant advertising boards.

With a chilly wind at our backs, we made our way further down into the valley, entering a residential sector where it opened up to reveal a large river with an ancient Roman bridge. At the start of the bridge, we looked straight ahead at a cliff face on the other side. A fifteenth-century castle graced the skyline, looming above all else. We crossed the river, turned left at the end of the bridge and meandered up to the medieval town above. We had only been on the road for five days since leaving Zamora but I needed to rest my leg, and this was a beautiful and interesting place to relax.

We entered the plaza where I sat with our gear on an ornate circular fountain while Mike, once again, went in search of accommodation. I watched people going about their daily tasks and conjured up the sights and sounds of the plaza centuries before. I see and hear a market brimming with noisy livestock, baskets of bread, colourful handmade clothing and jewellery, people bartering and enjoying the haggling, and maybe a maypole with children laughing and dancing to the strumming of a *mùsico callejero* (street musician). The sounds drifted away and were replaced by the tinkling of a bicycle bell. I heaved a deep sigh and turned my face to the sky to draw some warmth from the retreating afternoon sun.

Mike found a lovely boutique apartment nearby which was modern, warm and comfortable, and I was able to lie low for a couple of days with my foot up. I was hoping I would recover and be okay to walk into the mountains. After a couple of days of rest, we were back on the road, walking to Padornelo with the breeze blowing colder.

We had covered 732 kilometres and it would be only a few days until we entered Galicia. My leg was still playing up but it was bearable. The only place to stop that night was a hotel by the side of the main road that greeted us with spectacular views looking down and along a massive valley. The downside was the frustration of still not being able to find anything to eat that wasn't pork or cheese.

Being a vegetarian in Spain, where most meals include pork, was continuing to be a challenge, and I was so sick of cheese, cheese and more cheese. We hadn't seen green vegetables since we had started walking a month ago. We asked for vegetables in the restaurant that evening (I lived in hope) but there weren't any. I was over it.

On a brighter note, I sat and reflected on the other pilgrims we had met that morning: Josef and Lara, who were father and daughter, and Juan, a cyclist. They were all very friendly people. We had sat together in a café and chatted about one another's adventures. The sun shone through the front windows giving us feelings of warmth and relaxation before we headed out to meet the cold air once more. I really wasn't minding the cold that much, though. In fact, I was grateful for it. It was a little difficult to comprehend, given that we had been sweltering hot only weeks before. But positive thinking could sustain me only up to a certain point. I headed off to bed without dinner, which was not ideal, given I would need my energy for the next day.

Out on the highway the next morning, we came to a strip of small shops where we stopped at a store-come-café for some breakfast. We entered the dimly lit shop, which was cluttered from the bare wooden floorboards to the high wooden ceiling. Every wall, counter top, floor space and stand were crammed with an overload of merchandise. As I ran my eyes around the space adjusting to the light, I was confronted by the upper walls decorated with pig faces hung on small hooks that had been dried and stretched like masks. Mike asked me what I wanted as the assistant was waiting for us. I was still reeling and said, 'What?'

I walked outside to sit at the only table and two chairs that hugged the front of the building. I needed a few minutes to collect myself. I was still trying hard to get used to what was just a normal occurrence in our day. Not wanting to appear rude, I went back in avoiding anything higher than eye level. Mike had ordered coffees and a tortilla. While we waited, I looked further to see small brightly painted Spanish dolls, postcards, bull fighting posters, scarves, torches, leather bota bags (canteens), small dried pigs on stands, pig ears, cigarettes, cigars, sunglasses, leather gloves, caps embroidered with bulls, ceramic ornaments and mugs with images of bulls, large tins of olive oil with images of laden olive trees reminding me of Extremadura, cheeses by the dozens, sticks of bread and smoked hams hanging on larger hooks from a horizontal bar above the counter (which I didn't have a problem with).

In Melbourne, in the early 1970s, I had just taken over as manager of a gourmet delicatessen where one of my morning jobs was to chop up skinned rabbits to sell (which were popular with the older customers). One of the ladies always asked, 'Do you have a nice white piece of thigh, dear?' Sometimes, when I needed to go down in the basement to the walk-in freezer, it would freak me out when I opened the huge stainless-steel door as I didn't know what I was going to find lurking in there. One day, I reached up to put my hand in a box above me, and pulled out a little quail still covered with its feathers. I screamed and threw it into the air making for the door as quickly as I could, shaking all the way.

Another time, when on a working holiday in Britain, I worked in the deli of a prestige department store in Oxford Street, London. At Christmas time, when the pheasants were hung upside down to 'ripen' over the days, maggots would actually crawl from their eyes. I couldn't bear having them above the counter where we served customers and had to ask for them to be hung in an open fridge nearby.

I also remembered when, as a child visiting my grandparents on a weekend, they would choose a chook for dinner. We would trot off down to the pen, Papa would grab a chook by the legs holding it upside down with it squawking and flapping, chop its head off, give it to Mama to drain and clean. Then she and I would sit at the old concrete tubs where she would show me how to pluck it in readiness for the oven. It irked me but that was the way things were then and accepted as such. I began experimenting with becoming a pescatarian into my late forties and then it wasn't all at once. I would play with not eating meat for a couple of years and then go back to eating it for a while longer. By the time I was in my early fifties, I went 'cold turkey' and I don't miss it. It was a decision made for my sensitive gut issues but also an ethical one.

The next couple of days we encountered a lot of heavy rain, strong headwinds, hills and bitumen, and by the time we neared A Vilavella late one afternoon, we needed to make a decision about what path we would take, considering the conditions. Having walked many kilometres on the bitumen we didn't really want to navigate a mountain highway in rain and fog, but the alternative was a flooding Camino track with poor visibility and darkness approaching. We chose the highway, which was a little daunting given the size of the trucks and the narrowing of the road as we climbed.

Visibility became increasingly worse as the cloud moved in and the rain pelted down. We tried to protect our faces from the icy temperature and the lashing of the rain. At one point, we came to a curve in the road with a metal roadside barrier and a steep drop on the other side. We prayed that a truck wouldn't come around the corner. We couldn't walk on the other side of the road next to the rock wall because there was no shoulder on that side either. Just as I was thinking this, a massive truck approached. With the truck bearing down, we flattened the backs of our legs against the barrier and edged along the metal. Suddenly we came to a short gap in the barrier and we were able to jump and squeeze into the one-metre cavity. The truck roared past so close its force almost pulled us into it and gave us a further drenching. We wiped the water from our faces and looked at each other in total disbelief. 'Lucky,' said Mike.

We had been 'lucky' a number of times, and we felt 'looked after' yet again. I wasn't sure how long this stretch had taken us because my watch had stopped. It was already dusk and we needed to be off this mountain by dark. We eventually found our way down and across the highway, arriving in the old town of A Vilavella.

Mike

Arriving in the square of A Vilavella, we set our packs down next to the town well, which was ringed with steps. There was a noticeboard, but there was nothing I could see that mentioned any form of accommodation for the night. One of us needed to stay with our packs so I suggested I would reconnoitre on my own. We could see the sun clearly for the first time all day as it hurried towards the western horizon.

'I'll be back soon. I just want to walk around the town to see if I can find anything. I think I saw a large building in the distance on the way down. It was a castle maybe…or a large home? It's possibly a place to stay.'

A new highway bypassed A Vilavella which might explain why there appeared to be so little to offer visitors to this town. Once, shops, cafés and accommodation would have attracted people to stop, eat and rest, but the shops were now boarded up. I could hear the high-pitched sounds of cars and deep rumbling trucks in the distance. The town now appeared to be a collection of run-down houses facing concreted football and basketball courts. I met three teenage boys playing basketball and asked them if they knew of a hotel or an albergue.

They stared at me as if I was an alien, and one pointed and said (in Spanish), 'Over there near the service station – over the next hill. Not far.'

Fifteen or so minutes later, I arrived at a service station, and in the distance further up the hill I saw the large building I had seen earlier. After another ten minutes of walking, I was close enough to see that it was neither a castle nor a grand home. Its large car park was empty apart from one old Renault van of a type that seemed to be popular everywhere. A set of grand steps led up to a row of doors over which hung a faded sign: Hotel A Vilavella. The paint on the doors was peeling.

I was about to turn around and go back as the hotel looked as though it had been closed for ages, but I thought I might as well try the doors. I was surprised that they opened. Inside was a reception area with a large front desk, old sofas and a concierge's desk. It was silent and empty. Behind the front desk was a large row of shelves of empty pigeon holes each with room numbers painted on them. The front desk was bare except for a white sheet that lay draped over part of it. I could see that the surface was a richly textured wood and it would have once impressed guests with its size and presence. At the other end were steps with heavy bannisters that led up to the first floor. It felt as if this hotel had not heard the voices of guests for many years. There were faded sheets draped across armchairs. In another corner were dusty standing lamps and a coat stand. I could smell the mustiness and feel the iciness in the air on my cheeks.

When I called out – '*hola*' – I felt nervous that something scary might jump out from behind the sheeted furniture. I called again and waited. I was disappointed – *I had arrived ten years too late,* I thought. I decided to leave, but as I made my way out, I heard faint, muffled voices from behind a door at the back of the ghostly lobby. I walked across and gripped the handle and, for a brief moment hesitated, then ignored my fear and pushed it open.

It was like I had stepped through into another dimension. On the other side, I found a bar with scattered tables, half of them occupied by men playing cards or watching the football on the television. For the first time all day, I found myself in warmth, in the cosy company of people, and the possibility of a warm meal.

I went to the bar where the bartender greeted me and said that the hotel still operated, but the rooms had no heating or hot water because they hadn't been turned on in a while. He slid a key across the counter and invited me to have a look at a room, pointing to the stairs. One of the men at the table looked at me and tilted his head. '*Peregrino?*' He pointed at my wet Keens and held up the corner of his newspaper. I understood what he was trying to say and nodded: I could use newspapers to stuff into my shoes later as this would help dry them out.

With the key in my hand, I ventured deeper into the empty hotel. The floor was marble. There were brass fittings on the bannisters, heavy wooden tables and old sofas covered in sheets on each landing, waiting to come back to life. I was wet and I was aware of the cold stale air in the stairwells as I walked up three flights and down long, empty passageways until I found the room that corresponded to the number on my key. This place gave me the creeps. I would have returned the key and left, except – where would we stay?

I checked out the room then found my way back down to the bar. I asked the bartender about the cost and whether he could turn on the heating and the hot water. Why I asked about the cost I had no idea – it wasn't like I was going to check out the price anywhere else, it was just the force of habit. Making the booking didn't turn out to be so easy. For one thing, the bartender was reluctant to turn on the heating, because he would need to do it for the whole building. We got our wires crossed about what I wanted and I repeated that I wanted one room with two single beds, not two single rooms.

He went into the back room to find some paper and write it all down, including the cost. As I waited, I looked around at the men playing cards at the tables covered in fabric (green felt) and plates of chips and glasses of cognac or beer and it was like this was their evening ritual – quietly passing the time each night while the world had built a freeway and forgotten the town of A Vilavella. Apart from the man who showed me his newspaper, no one seemed to notice me. They were absorbed in their card games. The trials of the morning and my tiredness suddenly hit me and I was ready to fall into a bed, any bed, even the ancient sofa in the lobby. The bartender eventually reappeared with the figures written down and I assured him I would return shortly with my wife. With the booking finalised and a warm place to have dinner (and hopefully a warm room afterwards), I would have good news to share with Cici. I looked at my watch and realised I had lost track of time. Ordinarily, I don't lose track of the time. Ever.

Cici

As darkness fell, I stepped carefully on the cobblestone streets where cows (and what goes with cows) had obviously gone before. A few locals looked at me as they passed by and it was obvious they were wondering why I was there. A woman walked over to me and said something in Spanish. She spoke so quickly I couldn't comprehend what she was saying.

'I only speak English,' I said in Spanish. She walked away and stood next to a nearby building with another woman, maybe her neighbour, pointing at me and talking. A man came to sit on the step of a house diagonally opposite me as well.

As it became darker, I was feeling very vulnerable. Mike had been gone for ages, and panic was starting to set in. He had the bag with our passports, money and iPad, leaving me without identification, cash or communication. What if something had happened to him? I couldn't remember ever having felt so alone and scared.

The rain had stopped and the air was bitterly cold. I could see my breath escaping from my mouth and nostrils. The stone blocks of the well on which I had been sitting most of this time were very cold and hard. I tried to distract myself. I walked up the street a little to the church on the corner, still keeping the packs within my sight. The church was locked up. A couple of boys ran past yelling at each other in a playful way and bouncing a basketball. Life for them was business as usual. Their voices and the patter of the ball gradually disappeared into the distance and I felt alone again.

I walked back to the packs slowly – I didn't know how to pass the time or keep a lid on my emotions so I paced up and down, conscious of *el hombre* on the step and *las señoras* continuing their 'catch up' on the corner. I looked down at the drops of moisture clinging to my poncho and waterproof pants. *My shoes and socks had held up well in the downpour*, I thought to myself. As I reached for my gloves in the side of my pack, I felt a lump in my throat that was not going to be controlled. I tried to take deep breaths and hide my face from the world as my lips trembled and the involuntary tears fell like the rain on the mountain. This too couldn't be reined in; it was a force of nature and I could no longer deny my fatigue and panic. I had lost it and I didn't know which way to turn. I have always perceived myself as a strong, independent woman, but there was no way to reason with this.

The man who had been sitting on the step stood up and looked down the street. I turned to see a figure emerging from the darkness in the distance. As it came closer, I could see it was Mike. Sobbing hard but silently, I couldn't get the words out to tell him what was wrong. The man walked towards us, apparently checking that Mike and I were together and that I was okay. He mustn't have understood why I was alone and he had been sitting on the step looking out for me, yet I had mistaken his presence as loitering. Mike motioned to him that everything was okay. He mumbled numbly, 'Thanks mate, we're okay now.'

Mike kept repeating, 'I'm so sorry. I'm so sorry. I lost track of time.'

I cried into his shoulder, 'I thought something had happened to you. I was so scared. I had no way of calling you or anyone – I don't speak enough Spanish to be understood.'

We hugged at the well for some time as I cried out all the emotion. I felt childlike in his arms as he reassured me. We slowly put on our packs and walked hand-in-hand in silence towards the hotel.

Mike

Dinner was in the hotel's dining room (we were the only guests) and the barman appeared again, this time as our waiter. Cici and I hardly spoke over dinner as our bodies were exhausted and our emotions that welled up at the square had wrung any conversation out of us. Later, the patron in the bar gave me his sheets of newspaper, and by the time we returned to our room the heating had started to work.

Cici had a long bath and afterwards we lay together on one of the narrow beds. As I listened to her breathing, I thought about what she must have felt while I was gone. I had the passports and the money in my pack when I left her. My thoughts kept going round and round – how thoughtless I had been. She had no means of finding me or speaking to me and asking, 'Where are you? Are you okay?'

We are one another's lifeline and responsible for one another's wellbeing. Back home I can be casual about taking my time, but here I can't let 60 minutes slip by when I've said I am going to have a quick look around town. Yet, I was tired and had lost track of the minutes. I was determined to have our accommodation sorted before I returned to the square after our hellish day in the rain and cold to give her some good news.

A few days before we left for Spain, we picked Shirley up from residential care and took her to lunch at a restaurant by the sea. We each sat looking out over the water on that perfect blue sky day. Cici had instructed her to look after herself while we were gone. 'I will write to you as soon as we arrive in Spain, Shirl.' In her (sometimes) cranky voice, she shot back, 'Don't you worry about me, you make sure you look after each other.' She turned to me and said, 'You look after Cici now. Okay?'

Finding Cici in tears under the street light had cracked open feelings of tenderness within me. Instead of being annoyed with myself, all I felt now was love – my love for her filled me as I lay beside her on that small bed in that vast and empty hotel.

Cici

Waking the next morning, it was important to me to find some time for meditation and stillness so I could reflect on my distress of the previous night. I wrote in my journal about the range of emotions I had felt, and my love for my husband, family and friends. I never take love for granted – it is so precious. Many people go through life alone and unloved, and I had never been able to imagine – until now – what that might feel like. We phoned my son Thomas and daughter-in-law Simone; we hadn't spoken to them for more than a month. The phone reception was poor but it was lovely to hear their familiar voices. When we had to say goodbye, I realised how much I missed them.

Today would be a short walk of 14 sunny kilometres with a climb through shady oaks towards the next town, A Gudiña. We were leaving Extremadura and Castile and León behind and entering Galicia. On arriving in town, we spotted a café and ordered a late lunch of bean soup, crusty bread and coffee. We found a great albergue where we were the only occupants and had our choice of bunks. It was very clean, the heating was good, and there was space to wash some clothes that would dry on the windowsills.

Set high in the hills, the township of A Gudiña seemed to gracefully drape itself along the edge of the deep valley like the trim on a comfy armchair. We set out to explore the town and buy food for the next day, but we couldn't find a *supermercado* open on a Sunday. That was okay, we thought – we could shop for supplies tomorrow because we were no longer contending with the heat and didn't need to leave before dawn.

Sure enough, the next morning, after a coffee at the bar (no breakfast to be had) we came across a small grocery store. We couldn't find fresh bread other than some rolls lying on the floor behind the counter (not appealing) but bought two cans of sardines and some fruit. There was no other store so we started walking.

The walk out followed a steady incline. As we reached the highest pass we emerged from the fog and looked across at the distant mountains that formed the border with Portugal. Throughout the day the walking became harder with continual climbs and descents. I was pretty cranky about the pain in my leg and not having had enough to eat that morning.

To lighten the mood, Mike would yell out, 'Guess what's over that hill?' and I would yell back, 'Another hill!' to which he responded, 'Correct!' This became a standing joke.

There were three villages shown on the map, which gave me hope of food (and someone to say, 'Hi!' to), but they all turned out to be very old and small, and didn't have a bar or shop between them. We saw some beautiful scenery below the ridge and then descended into the town of Campobecerros.

Again, we arrived during siesta and there was not a soul around as we walked up the narrow cobblestone alleyways searching for our night's stay. We found the albergue surprisingly modern and clean, if very small, which was not a problem given the few pilgrims on the trail. Our only companion that night was Miguel, a lovely Spanish cyclist. I noticed a stack of blankets in the corner, which was a welcome sight since we had posted our sleeping bags home weeks before. This albergue, like some others, provided disposable paper bed sheets. I was starting a little collection of my used ones so I could have a top sheet as well.

There wasn't a lot to explore in this little town, but we witnessed a breath-taking sunset where the radiating soft silver-blue light highlighted the lush green fields. The wooden fence posts of the farms and herds of grazing goats formed silhouettes against the horizon. That evening we enjoyed a drink at the bar nearby, and I saw something that made my eyes pop out on stalks: in walked a woman carrying a small basket containing about a dozen eggs. The basket was open-weave so there was no mistaking them (you may gather we hadn't seen eggs for a long time). I watched as she walked around the back of the bar to the kitchen area. I told Mike we should let the lady at the bar know we would like eggs for dinner and between us we conjured up enough Spanish to ask.

'*Sin huevos*' ('We have no eggs'), she replied.

Hmmm, I thought, *they are keeping them close to their chest.*

'But I saw them walking around the bar in a basket,' I said in my poor Spanish. At that point, Miguel joined us and I told him with some excitement what we had seen. I probably sounded quite desperate by that point. Thankfully, Miguel intervened on our behalf. By the time dinner was served, the kitchen had found the non-existent eggs and the three of us enjoyed an egg each with chips and bread. We were very grateful to Miguel. We strolled back in the cold mist, hung our socks to dry, stuffed our boots and shoes with newspaper, and snuggled into our bunks with our thermals, beanies and cosy blankets. '*Buenas noches, Miguel*,' we wearily said to our friend. It was a good night.

The next morning we met Miguel in the bar for coffee and breakfast. He asked for some food for the journey and was told there wasn't any available. There wasn't anywhere else open at this time. We hadn't been able to find a supermarket the day before, either. Our faces dropped. Miguel told the owners he had to ride many challenging hills that day and needed some food. Mike and I had an apple and a few nuts in our packs but not enough to sustain us through the hills. All the bar could give us for breakfast were a few slices of teacake and one orange juice, which Miguel drank. Mike and I started out with only our few leftovers from the previous day. We were grateful we had fewer kilometres to walk today. We said a heartfelt goodbye to Miguel, wishing him '*Buen Camino*'.

It was a very cold minus two degrees Celsius, but this climbed to five degrees quite quickly as we set out. We were heading for Laza. I had been looking forward to this day since I started researching the Camino because we would reach one of the most profound and significant, if modest, landmarks of the Vía de la Plata. We soon arrived at that point on the roadside near Portocambo where the monks of Los Milagros had erected a sixteenth-century cross. It was made from chestnut wood to honour the pilgrims of the past and the present. I wished specifically to honour the pilgrim who had perished in the heat on our route a few weeks before we started, and another Japanese pilgrim who had died in freezing conditions on the Camino Francés while we were walking in the heat.

I had written a blessing to read at the cross, and laid one of the hand-held wooden crosses from my workplace of St John of God on the stones near the base of the cross alongside messages left by other pilgrims. The hand-held wooden cross was carved by Gary, who was one of the volunteers at the Frankston Men's Shed, Victoria, while he was recovering from a serious illness. Carving the crosses for the hospital had given him a renewed sense of purpose and meaning in life. This was a special moment for me because I was walking this particular Camino in honour of St John of God. After his death, in 1550 at the age of 55, his followers formed the order of the Brothers Hospitallers of St

John of God. He was canonised in the seventeenth century, and the hospitals continue his mission in the community globally. The Camino Francés in the north has an equivalent landmark of religious significance, the enormous Iron Cross of St James, where people stop to pray and leave a blessing and a stone or something similar.

As we slowly made our way down the range, my leg was increasingly bothersome, but the best thing to do was to keep it to myself for the time being and not complain. There hadn't been anywhere I could see a doctor for five days.

Mike

The next couple of days we continued into the mountains walking in sight of the border with Portugal. We climbed steadily each day and our shoes were tested over the uneven, mostly rock-strewn paths. I was onto my second pair of Keens. One of Cici's shoes had fallen apart and we regretted not packing duct tape.

That day we walked from A Gudiña to Campobecerros – it was hard going and the gradient was steep. In the distance, we could see mountain ranges that we had read were the border with Portugal. Against the cobalt blue sky, the outline of the mountains was like a drawing against a blue watercolour background. Our bodies were tired and each time I stubbed my toes the pain would shoot up and jar my spine. Cici was experiencing pain down her leg at nine on a scale of one to ten and was walking in silence, leaning on her walking poles instead of holding them lightly. My too-frequent questions – 'How are you feeling?' 'How is it going?' – were being ignored. She reminded me how annoying I could be. I kept a buffer of a couple of hundred metres between us and left her to her own company occasionally looking back to make sure she hadn't stopped at the side of the trail.

We arrived in a village at the top of the ridgeline with hopes of finding a café – a taverna would have been heaven! But as we walked down the main road it looked abandoned. There were some houses but they were mostly falling down, and yet a few farm animals and vegetable patches suggested that some people still lived here. We saw no one.

We were hungry so we decided to rest and set ourselves down on a low stone wall opposite a row of abandoned semi-detached houses. The veranda that ran the length of the row had collapsed. Walking through villages like this was like walking through the past and the present at the same time. This one was empty and there was no sound of human life, but I could picture how it had been. Once,

I imagined, it would have been a community where people cared for their small farms, kept animals and where they met at the local café, where they gossiped and celebrated festivals and where children played. Did the children grow up and go to the city to find work? Did the parents move into aged care or join their children some place a world away from the peace here? Gradually the life and the noise of the village would have fallen silent and the houses decayed. Strangers took away the furnishings and fittings, leaving the birds to make nests in the living room. The roofs caved in.

I sat on the broken-tiled floor of one of the rooms and looked at the open sky through the hole where the roof had once been. I looked through the window of what had once been the kitchen. I could see a field of yellow canola in the valley below. The view had probably not changed since the last occupant had looked out the window, perhaps holding a coffee and contemplating his or her future. Now a flowering vine had grown up the walls, reaching up to the sky where the roof once was. There was a cycle of life here: people grew up, then left, but life returned as these empty houses were taken over by vines, flowers and nests.

Many more hills later, we arrived in Campobecerros after lunch. We checked into the albergue and met Miguel, a *peregrino* from Madrid, who was doing the Camino on his bicycle. He was a trim man in his forties with an open, likeable manner. Like a few *peregrinos* we had met, he shared a story of a life-changing event. He had suffered partial blindness after an industrial accident in which a glass beaker exploded, shooting tiny fragments into his eye and permanently damaging his optical nerve. When I asked him about his family, he showed me a photo of his young son, a happy six-year-old wearing a football jumper – a Real Madrid fan. When Miguel talked about his son, he put his hand on his heart and smiled.

We were the only three people staying in the albergue. I was lying on my bunk when Miguel called from outside where he was standing on the back stairs looking at a lunar phenomenon. 'Ven a ver la luna!' ('Come see the moon!') Around the world, the 'supermoon' shone brightly that night. It hung in the sky like a silver coin and the roof tops and hills were bathed in the softest of blue lights. I remember reading that in the Middle Ages, travellers followed the celestial path of the moon and the Milky Way all the way to Santiago. Like a carpet of stars it would have reassured and guided them like a map pointing them to their destination.

That night I had a dream. It was a version of Charles Dickens' *A Christmas Carol*. In the dream, I was Scrooge and I was doing the Camino. I was reviewing the past few weeks, the hot boring days in Extremadura, the cold wet days in Galicia, and all the time I was whining about the food. I was visited by the ghost of 'Christmas Yet to Come', who reminded me of my old school headmaster. He was wearing his black academic gown and his usual scowl. He pointed at me with his bony finger and delivered a stern rebuke: 'Get a grip!' Then he granted me a second chance – at what? I was not sure, for at this point I woke up from the dream.

For breakfast, we returned to the same bar where we'd eaten dinner the night before. There was little on offer to inspire us. There was beer, however. Two patrons in the corner were already getting a jump on the challenges of the day and working through their glasses of *cerveza*. Miguel drank the last bottle of juice and the woman at the bar put a couple of slices of teacake on the counter. This would have to do for breakfast. It was time to go our separate ways, and Cici and I took turns hugging Miguel and wishing him *'Buen Camino'*. I felt a lump in my throat when it was my turn.

'Take care! Go well, my friend! May God take care of you! *Buen Camino*!'

The mornings were now so cold I was wearing my fleece, vest, rain jacket and gloves. Once we had found our rhythm of walking, I told Cici about my dream.

'I think it means I can change the way I think about this Camino. I have a second chance.' I told her again that so far, I had not been fully present on our trek. I had been caught up in my thoughts, just wanting to get through the days and not really being there. Cici had always been closer to the direct experience of it all, even if that meant being in pain. There were times when she stopped to notice the small flowers on the path while I was unaware of their existence.

'Quick, come back and take a look at this,' she would say. 'Of what?'

'Of all the little purple flowers you've been walking over.'

I continued reflecting aloud on my dream.

'I just want to be more present to it all. I want to feel it more, like you seem to do. I don't know what happens to the feelings I experience; I just seem to be really good at pushing them away or down.'

I knew a big part of my resistance came from being in survival mode. If I felt everything about the Camino, I would go into emotional overload. You have to 'suck it up' so you can push yourself through all of the relentless walking, the hardship and the monotony. But if I was good at suppressing what I felt about the hard parts, did I also suppress the feelings at the other end of the spectrum? What about feelings like wonderment? Joy? The previous evening, looking at the night sky and the supermoon, I tried to think of what I felt. I'd taken photos and marvelled. But was there a feeling? I couldn't remember feeling anything. I only remember what I felt long ago when I sometimes looked up at the moon. I had a memory of feeling moved when I was in school catching the train home one evening. I had stood on the station platform looking at the horizon after the sun had set and had seen the autumn sky turn to dark blue and then black. I saw a crescent moon and then the distant star of Venus. What was it I'd felt then? It was a feeling of ecstasy, a quiet joy. Awe.

The message in the *Christmas Carol* dream was that it was possible for me to have a different experience of the Camino. Maybe it was still possible to be more present in the moment and to experience feelings I had not felt in many years. I still had time. Just like Scrooge in the story who still got to experience Christmas, I had ten days of walking to go before we arrived in Santiago. This insight lifted my spirits and I walked on, quickly finding my rhythm. Happy and excited now, I enjoyed the feeling of the sun warming my gloveless hands.

Meanwhile, Cici's pain had returned, making the walking uphill difficult. She needed to see someone about her leg and foot. She has an old injury from her marathon running days – a stress fracture – and we were concerned she had aggravated the injury. If this was true, then it would be very difficult for us to continue without a lengthy rest break – maybe weeks, not days. Our goal now was to walk to Laza, where we knew there was a medical clinic.

Later in the morning we walked through a small village where a Camino devotee had set up a self-serve food and drink bar under the overhang of the second story of his or her stone house. It was all very makeshift, but in a charming way. Jars of biscuits, a thermos of hot water, instant coffee and tea bags were placed on a table made from what looked like driftwood, with two branches arranged to form a ledge on which sat a bowl of mandarins. A plate held bits of coloured chalk that *peregrinos* had used to write their names and home countries on the stone wall of the ground level of the house. There were messages and greetings from South America, New York, New Zealand and Japan, and I realised a stream of travellers from all over the world had passed through this road-side kiosk. As we left, I saw a large yellow hand-painted sign with the words 'Laza 6 kilometres' and an arrow pointing to the right. It was a relief to know we could be at a medical clinic by midday.

Laza is a small town with a square bordered by a clinic, a pharmacy and a café-restaurant. We were hungry, having eaten only a slice of teacake each for breakfast, and some arrowroot biscuits and two mandarins at the self-serve stop with the colourful chalk messages. We debated whether to go to the doctor first or have a *bocadillo* at the café. Cici was in such pain we decided the food could wait.

Fortunately, a doctor was rostered that day and could see her immediately, and I stayed in the waiting room to keep an eye on our gear. After a while, I realised our gear was safe where it was, and I wandered into the consulting room to hear the doctor summing up his advice. He was a portly man, who reminded me of the actor Brian Dennehy. He was casually dressed in a white doctor's coat with open necked shirt and slippers. In the corner, sat a young nurse. Cici sat in the middle of the room. Speaking in a raised voice, he was stabbing with his pen at a drawing of her leg on his jotter pad to emphasise his point. The nurse translated: 'Doctor says your leg is very bad. Yes, it is very bad and you must rest now. No more Camino. You must not walk. He says you must not walk anymore.'

The doctor repeated this and kept pointing at his drawing of Cici's leg. He also pointed accusingly down at her left shoe, which was now peeling open like a banana. 'Very bad,' he said. I don't recall whether his warning had anything to do with her old stress fracture. The exact consequences of continuing to walk were not spelt out, but the message was pretty clear: no more walking for Cici!

We collected our gear and went to the chemist next door to buy a support bandage and wait for the painkillers the doctor had prescribed. We sat in stunned silence taking in what the doctor had said and what it meant. Should we just stop? We had been hoping to have lunch and push on that afternoon but now it seemed we would be waiting here while she recovered. The doctor's stern message suggested that a few days would not be long enough. Then the nurse who had translated for the doctor came to ask us what we were going to do. She offered to drive us to Ourense, 50 kilometres away.

'Really, you can do that for us?'

'Yes, the doctor said I could leave early and I should take you to Ourense.'

Sonya, the nurse, drove us via the scenic route, perhaps to cheer us up after the bad news. She gave us a running commentary on the features of the towns as we flew past them. I hadn't been in a car for weeks and Sonya liked to drive fast (she was nudging 120 kilometres on the freeway), so within a short while I was car sick. I found it hard to appreciate the towns she showed us and especially difficult to pay attention after the roundabouts, which she barely slowed down for. Looking straight ahead at the road while trying to take my mind off my heaving stomach, I asked her about her family and her life. Sonya lived on a small farm with her husband, her daughter and two animals, a pig and a donkey. I was grateful for her generosity in taking us to Ourense, and I was even more grateful to get out of the car when she dropped us off near the city centre.

Within an hour, we lay resting on comfortable beds in a hotel. As I stared at the ceiling, I could hear the sounds of the city through the open window – cars honking, buses rumbling, the tweeting of a pedestrian crossing turning green and the familiar buzz of city life. Thoughts raced through my mind. Would Cici recover to finish the Camino? I couldn't help wondering about my dream and if I would have another chance to walk the Camino differently.

Cici

Everything was flickering by so fast that I was starting to feel nauseated as well. We hadn't eaten, so Sonya dropped us outside a café in Ourense, saying goodbye and wishing us well. Ourense was a large city, so Mike had already booked a hotel with the expectation we would arrive in two days' time. He rang to see if there was a vacancy for that night. Luckily, he was able to book the last available room.

Later sitting on the bed next to Mike – both of us still reeling from the sequence of events that morning – I was amazed at the list of positive thoughts that were lining up in my mind. First, there had actually been a doctor in attendance in Laza, which is only a very small town. Second, the pharmacy had been open so I could buy the medication I needed. If we'd arrived ten minutes later, it would have been closed. Third, it was the only day of the week that Sonya – who, importantly for us, spoke English – worked in Laza. Fourth, she was able to leave work early so she could drive us to Ourense, which meant we didn't need to wait until the end of the day for a bus. Fifth, we had booked the last available room at the hotel and we wouldn't need to move later to another hotel or another room. And finally, Ourense had stores where I could buy a new pair of shoes. I knew we were being looked after.

We passed near this church, Ermita de la Virgen del Castillo,
on the way to Montamarta.

A familiar and reassuring Camino marker en route to Campobecerros.

A brief communion with a
local burro.

Miguel and his wife offered
wonderful hospitality at their
restaurant El Mona in Villanueva
de las Peras.

Walking through fog on the road
to A Vila Vella.

In A Gudiña, we had the pilgrim
hostel all to ourselves, for five
euros per person.

Cici often imagined the life that once existed in abandoned villages such as this one near Laza.

Brien Crothers, a fellow peregrino,
inspired us with the idea of 'tu
Camino' (your Camino).

At siesta time, the main street of the town of Granja de Moreruela was deserted.

As dog lovers, we were sometimes saddened by the sight of (apparently) abandoned dogs in the countryside.

A refreshment stand offering hot drinks and biscuits to pilgrims on the way to Laza.

One of the cafés we spent time at in Zamora.

Arriving at the chestnut cross at Portocambo and leaving a hand-carved cross from St John of God hospital in Melbourne at its base.

The bridge to the medieval town of Puebla de Sanabria with Castillo de los Condes de Benavente in the background.

The Ponte Vella bridge, Ourense.

Between A Gudiña and Campobecerros, we stopped for a break at a row of abandoned houses.

The streets and laneways of Mike's favourite city, Ourense,
were perfect for meandering.

Walking from A Vila Vella, the morning greeted us with the lush beauty of the woods.

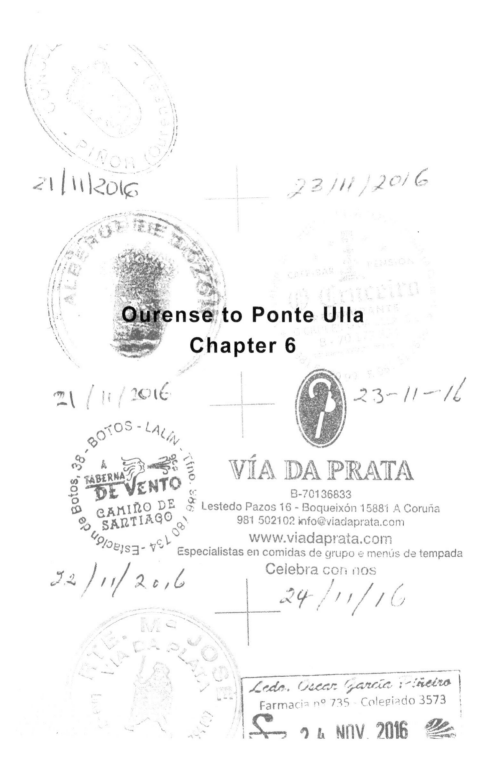

21/11/2016

23/11/2016

Ourense to Ponte Ulla
Chapter 6

21 / 11 / 2016

23-11-16

VÍA DA PRATA
B-70136833
Lestedo Pazos 16 - Boqueixón 15881 A Coruña
981 502102 info@viadaprata.com
www.viadaprata.com
Especialistas en comidas de grupo e menús de tempada
Celebra con nos

22/11/2016

24/11/16

Ledo. Oscar García Piñeiro
Farmacia nº 735 - Colegiado 3573
2 4 NOV. 2016

Kindred Spirits

Cici

During our time in Ourense I bought a pair of walking shoes and a battery for my watch, and we had our credentials stamped at the cathedral where I spent quite a while admiring the life-size carved stone statues of the saints, including St James. My mind was constantly returning to the Camino as I felt guilty for not having walked the last 53 kilometres. I was trying to work out how to go back to Laza. I found out the buses didn't go every day, and when they did, it was not at times that would allow us to get our day-time walking in. Realistically though, I needed to take time out, as I didn't want to jeopardise our last 100 kilometres.

'Let it go,' Mike kept reminding me. I was trying to honour the Camino in the best way possible. It wasn't about ego. I didn't need to be seen as conquering it or smashing it. I know it was never a part of my agenda, if I had one. I have been told a few times that I am a perfectionist. This trait had obviously shown up here. When committing to anything in life, I feel I need to put my heart and soul into it, whether professionally or personally; otherwise, I don't see the point. This is who I am.

When I was about seven years old, I decided I wanted to go to Sunday School. I didn't know exactly what it was, but I wanted to check it out. Mum and Dad didn't attend church – in fact, religion was not on their radar – so when I brought up the subject of wanting to go, they asked how I was going to get there.

Dad would be mowing the lawn and Mum would be cooking a roast for lunch and looking after my younger brothers and sisters. I said I would take myself, but I would need a pair of gloves and a hat; otherwise I felt I couldn't go. In those days, women and girls were required to cover their heads to attend church or Sunday School. Everything was so formal then. I wanted to be like the other girls in school and so I needed to wait a few weeks until Mum and Dad could come up with the goods – it had to be perfect.

My hat looked like a beehive. It had white netting with yellow flowers perched in the dip at the top. I wore white lace gloves decorated with a little pearl button on the inside of my wrist, black patent shoes, and my good blue dress with a ruffle and a sash, and I carried a pale blue patent handbag. Off I walked, feeling equipped and ready to meet this man called Jesus that everyone spoke of.

When I arrived home, Dad asked, 'So did you meet the boogie man?'

Mum replied for me, 'Noel, just let her be. If she wants to go, just let her.'

However, I did meet Father Thompson, who called me Bluebell. Father gave me an attendance stamp (similar to a postage stamp) which I stuck in my attendance book every week. Each stamp depicted a religious image. At Christmas and Easter, the stamps were larger and beautifully coloured. Maybe this is why I loved having my pilgrim credentials stamped on the Camino. A few years later when I started going to church in preparation for my confirmation, Father Beer,[8] a young cleric, appeared on the scene – he regularly roared into the grounds of St Margaret's Church on his motorbike, complete with leather jacket and boots. I was then hooked on going to church.

I experienced a couple of emotional days in Ourense working out whether to return to Laza to make up the kilometres we hadn't walked, but eventually I came to accept that my injury was part of this experience. We took time out to soak in the thermal springs and sauna (but not too for long for me), visited the monastery, the impressive albergue and history museum next door, and saw a

---

[8] I spoke with Father Beer in the early part of 2020 after he had just celebrated his 80th birthday.

physiotherapist a few times. We ambled through the streets taking in the culture, walked on another amazing Roman bridge and ate great food. One night, standing in the centre of the bridge, we watched the supermoon rise from behind the mountains, its golden shape reflected in the dark river below.

The next day we posted another parcel of belongings home. We were down to the basics for the next week. I had my last physio appointment, which involved having my leg taped, and Mike and I talked about walks we would like to do along the Great Ocean Road in Victoria the following year – we were setting goals for the future. Our bodies were feeling ready to embark on the last 100 kilometres and we were looking forward to it. Both of us felt we would like to do things differently. Mike, remembering his dream, was going to try different ways of being as he walked. He wanted to be accepting of everything that was thrown his way. For me, I wanted to receive 'the path' more graciously.

Mike

I welcomed the time in Ourense. I was attracted to this city immediately. I loved the look and feel of it there – I loved the older parts and the modern sections that were separated and connected by a series of bridges across the wide Minho River. I happily meandered, wanting to stay more than the four days we had planned. Unlike Cici, I enjoyed indulging myself a little in this city.

I spent one afternoon soaking in the outdoor heated mineral pools that were a short walk from the Roman bridge, the Ponte Vella. Soaking in the warm waters, I could feel myself relax and I experienced a deep level of tiredness in my body and mind. Afterwards, we slowly walked back to our hotel via the Ponte Vella, where we rested at the centre of the span and looked across to the mountains in the distance, knowing that Santiago lay beyond them. The bridge became a favourite spot for me, I found it relaxing looking out meditatively on the river from this high point. I thought it was amazing that we had come this far. I wondered what sorts of challenges the last 100 kilometres would present us with.

On our last night in Ourense, we ate dinner across the road from our hotel. I was keen to put my concerns for Cici's injuries out of my mind and enjoy our last night here experiencing more of the food for which Galicia is famous. We were the only patrons for the first couple of hours as we still turned up for dinner at the ungodly early hour of 7.30 pm. The owner lavished us with attention. The items on the menu were a bit inscrutable, so we asked him to bring us a range of dishes. He brought each sharing plate with a flourish of the hand and a detailed explanation of the dish. I ended up eating more than my share as Cici couldn't eat the meat (and we didn't want to offend our host). We consumed more than our normal volume of wine as we were generously offered various samples from the cellar. I felt very jolly at the end of the night and tipped the owner 50 euros, but he was embarrassed and refused to accept it. I remember giggling a lot as we crossed the road with Cici steering me towards the hotel.

The next morning it was raining heavily, which was not uncommon for Galicia at this time of year. It had been good having a break from our packs and from carrying our poles during the past few days, but it also felt exciting to be back on the journey, especially now that we were so close to Santiago.

A fun-run event was being held that morning in the city and for the first hour we walked against the flow of joggers in their bright T-shirts and coloured plastic ponchos. On the roadside, hawkers sold squid from large pots that simmered on gas burners. We stopped for a *café con leche* on the edge of the city and then walked on past the industrial estates, along the freeway and finally into the forest. The many shades of green and the elm trees turning to autumn colours were so unlike the grey, dusty, flat landscape with the ubiquitous squat holm oaks we had experienced in Extremadura.

We walked down country roads and gravel paths carpeted in autumn leaves and across stone bridges spanning small rivers. I felt optimistic now we were back on track, walking side by side again. I started to wonder how it would feel when we finally walked into Santiago. I tried to imagine how Cici would feel. Would she feel a sense of achievement? Would it all be worth it?

We talked about Dan and Lea – how we missed their companionship and not being able to share our experiences with them. It had been a couple of weeks since they had returned to Saskatchewan following the death of Dan's sister. I wondered how they were managing back home. By mid-afternoon, we were about five kilometres from our next albergue. The clouds had cleared and some sun was appearing. We walked in silence along the highway where we were overtaken by a bus from Ourense. As it passed, I saw the destination sign in its rear window and read it out loud.

'Santiago!'

It was becoming real! We were so close! Barring some injury or mishap, nothing could stop us now! The bus pulled into a stop up ahead and then pulled out again. We saw a couple of walkers now standing where the bus had been. They hoisted their packs onto their backs. Two people like us!

'Hola! Hello!' called Cici.

'Oh no!' called back one of the pair, a bearded man. 'You have caught us cheating! We caught the bus!'

Eva and Göran were Swedes, and both were veterans, having walked many Caminos. After introductions, we walked on together to our destination for the night, the village of Cea. Upon arriving at the albergue, Cici, Eva and Göran headed off into the village with the manager of the albergue, who guided them to a bakery that sold the bread this town was famous for. I stayed back to dry off my shoes and socks. I remembered what the fellow at the bar in A Vilavella had said and I went in search of old newspapers.

That night was the first of five in the company of our new Camino companions. Over the following days as we walked together, we found ourselves laughing and sharing Camino stories. Cici and I seemed to have discovered the lighter side of life again. We introduced Eva and Göran to our afternoon ritual where I, keeper of the lollies, would dole out jelly babies, and blackberry and raspberry jubes. They laughed and laughed, with Eva saying, 'This is so wonderful.'

One afternoon we sat side by side on a stone wall eating our lunch of Portuguese sardines and bread. Behind us in a paddock a goat was bleating mournfully. Göran pointed out that the goat sounded like he was calling out for someone called Erik. We all paused for a moment to listen and then erupted in laughter as we heard Erik's name being called. At the time, it seemed to be the funniest thing.

Later that day, Cici learned that Eva was frightened of the dogs in Spain so she taught her how to do her 'scary bear' routine by standing up to her full height on her toes, with arms and fingers outstretched above her head. This was accompanied by lots of growly sound effects. It took a few practises for Eva to get the routine right with Cici assessing her scariness and giving her tips while Göran and I watched and applauded.

In only a couple of days, the Camino had become filled with this gentle humour and silliness. But I also learned stuff from Göran. As a wiser and more experienced pilgrim than me, one of the things he taught me was that the whole Camino experience is enhanced when one takes little detours. For example, one should always pause when the opportunity arises to enter a local bar.

Enlightenment, he advised, could not be attained without inspiration from full strength beer. Light beer would not do. I soon learned that tavernas were just as important as cathedrals when it came to landmarks on the pilgrim's journey. How was it, I wondered, that Göran was able to down a pint of *cerveza* and then power on for the rest of the afternoon, while I struggled to keep up with him. I soon abandoned my habit of only one glass of red with dinner.

On our third day, together we came upon a tavern where we had a pit stop and refuelled. It was a small village watering hole fronted by large empty oak barrels that served as tables. Entering and stepping down into the interior was like entering a cave. My eyes took a few moments to adjust to the darkness and the simple rustic interior. There was the overpowering smell of smoke and cooking odours.

After ordering, we returned outside into the sunlight and sat around a barrel. Göran drank his pint of beer, Eva drank non-alcoholic beer and Cici stuck to her water, and we took snaps of ourselves on our phones. It was a beautiful warm autumn afternoon and I realised I was happy. This was how I had imagined it would be. This was the vision I had carried of the 'ideal' Camino experience – sitting with new friends and sharing this journey together.

Earlier I mentioned Cea, a historically important town, where we had first spent a night with Eva and Göran. We had also shared the albergue there with a small group of exuberant Spanish pilgrims. Our plan now was to arrive at the next town ahead of that group in case we could get rooms that offered some privacy. Some albergues have smaller rooms away from the open dormitory, which you can snaffle if you arrive first. After our stop at the tavern, we quickened our pace to get there first as planned. We arrived to find a modern building with comfortable-looking facilities (we could see them through the windows). Unfortunately, it was locked up.

We pushed on to the next town, Dozón, hoping the albergue there would be just as nice. The weather was colder now. Only a month ago we had been racing to beat the energy-sapping afternoon sun. Now we were hurrying to arrive before the cold and the icy rain set in. Along the way we found things to make us laugh, like local farm animals: the curious cows, the melancholic donkeys and the pigs that the Spanish love so much for the cured ham. We took photos of the pigs and greeted them cheerfully (*'Hola, Señor Jamón!'*). Cici still found the smell of pig excrement off-putting (but nothing like the smell of it in the heat), unlike Eva. 'I don't mind it really,' she said, 'it smells like the country.'

We settled into two private rooms in our albergue in Dozón. We were delighted to find a cupboard full of spare blankets and we each grabbed a couple. The nights now had quite a bite. The large communal area upstairs would accommodate our Spanish friends. We wandered back to the village to find some food for dinner. With the light fading, the sky had turned a wintery ice blue and the moon was visible on the horizon. Further up the road we saw the Spanish pilgrims approaching, filing slowly into town. I raised my hand to slap high fives and they each slapped it gently in turn as they passed me, tired but smiling. It was a moment of warmth and connection.

Loaded up with food, we returned to the albergue's large commercial-style kitchen to prepare our dinner: spicy sausage and bread, followed by poached fish and greens. While Göran and I set the table with white plates from the cupboards, Göran took out his Swiss Army pocketknife and began sharpening the main blade. He flipped over a china saucer and ran the blade back and forth over the raised lip on the base, grinding the knife's edge into the china. Within moments, Eva called out from the kitchen.

'What's that awful noise? Stop it, Göran! Stop it!'

Göran looked at me, puzzled, and continued sharpening his knife. Then both Cici and Eva called out together, 'Stop it! It's like fingernails on a blackboard! We can't stand it!'

Göran grinned. 'What sound? Oh, that sound! But I like that sound! I find it relaxing.'

He continued to grind away into the china with his knife. I instantly recognised it as a game I play with Cici. Don't ask me why I do it, it is just one of those things I find funny and endearing about our relationship. Certain sounds I find meditative, like the sounds of ticking clocks, which she finds stressful and sends her into a flurry of agitation. Once I set our three loud clocks going, I sit back and wait until Cici rushes out of her study where she has been concentrating on something like writing a long email.

'What is that noise? How can you put up with that racket?'

And that's when I typically respond, 'But I like that sound! It relaxes me!'

Göran plays the same game with Eva.

That night in the dining room we couldn't get the heaters working so we ate dinner wearing our coats and beanies. Afterwards, we washed the dishes together, drying the plates and cutlery and putting them away, and filled up the bins with our empty wine bottles. At one point, I jokingly pulled Göran's beard and we ended up laughing as we looked at one another with washing suds on our chins and noses. In that moment, I had become a younger version of myself, like the boy who once enjoyed being silly and who could feel awe at the sight of the moon and the first star appearing in the sky.

Cici

Walking from Ourense to Cea meant walking 21 kilometres in heavy rain, but fortunately it was not too cold. It was still raining as we arrived on the outskirts late in the afternoon with our new Swedish companions and walked through the narrow, winding cobblestone streets to find the albergue. The manager, Orlando, was tall and dark, with an impressive moustache. We checked in, had our credentials stamped, found our bunk and then attempted to convey to Orlando in Spanish that we needed a *supermercado*.

'There is no supermarket here and everything except the bar is now closed,' he replied in his broad Spanish accent.

I guess he felt sorry for us because he made a call on his mobile and asked us to follow him. Eva, Göran and I stopped behind Orlando outside a bakery with a massive old wooden door. A lady answered Orlando's knock and welcomed us into her shop with its aged shelves, flooring and equipment. There was one loaf left of Cea's famous bread, which we bought to share – yay! We thanked her so much for her hospitality and said our goodbyes. Orlando motioned for us to follow him.

As we walked through the now darkening laneways, he indicated we were passing his home and then led us on to our next stop, a tiny bar with a small scattering of locals on stools staring at yet another gathering of foreigners calling themselves *peregrinos*. Orlando made conversation with his friends while he waited for us to buy a couple of bottles of red. I bought an extra bottle for Orlando to thank him for his help, but he wouldn't accept it.

Back at the albergue we all scratched around in our packs for odd bits of food, placing a few pieces of fruit, a can of sardines, a small block of cheese and a piece of smoked chorizo along with our dark, crusty loaf of fresh bread in the centre of the long wooden table. Orlando found some cups for the wine. We sat and paused, smiling at each other as we scanned our shared goodies then toasted Orlando. I offered a blessing for our newfound friendships and Orlando's care, and gratitude for the modest meal set before us. The spell of this special moment of connectedness was broken by the sound of a slamming door and loud excited voices – the Spanish pilgrims had arrived! The eating and laughing began.

That night we were thankful for our warm, dry beds, having walked all day in the rain and cold with wet shoes and socks. We slept soundly while our boots and socks dried near the heaters.

In the morning, Mike and I headed off earlier than the others to have our coffee in the bar I had visited the night before. We found the same group of locals either perched on stools or folded into round-backed chairs staring from beneath the peaks of their damp caps at the pilgrims entering their sacred watering hole. '*Buenos días*,' I said as we entered and was met with varying nods. We ate *tostadas de tomate* layered with olive oil and sea salt, and drank the much-anticipated *café con leche*.

Before we left, I asked about the bathroom. The *señora* behind the bar beckoned to one of the older men, Antonio, who sat hunched in the corner, to show me the way. I followed him out the front door and around the side of the building. He motioned for me to stop and not to go through the open door to the bathroom. I stood looking on, curious, as he ran water and soap into a bucket, grabbed a rag lying on the ground and began washing the toilet bowl and surrounds. I looked on in amazement. When he appeared to have finished, he stood and looked at me and motioned again for me not to enter. He then grabbed another cloth and proceeded to wipe the area dry. I became quite emotional. He replaced the bucket and rag on the nearby well and waved for me to enter. As he did, our eyes met and we nodded to each other.

When I returned to the bar, Antonio was seated with his back to me. From behind, I gently placed my hand on his shoulder. Without looking up he placed his hand over mine and nodded, still looking down at the floor. The lady behind the bar noticed us, but she said nothing, and neither did the others. Mike looked perplexed. We swung our packs onto our backs, buckled up and left. As we began our walk through the village past the town fountain where locals were collecting fresh water in buckets and jugs, tears streamed down my face. If nothing else extraordinary happened on this pilgrimage, then that would be totally okay.

'Tell me when you are ready,' Mike said.

I explained what Antonio had done for me. I was in awe of the profound power of such a simple act of care and respect. To experience kindness in that way is a touching of souls. I was very reflective all day and needed to be in silence.

179

As we continued on to Dozón, the mercury didn't reach more than eight degrees Celsius and the rain pelted down. On arriving, we found coffee and fresh doughnuts at a café-bar then made our way to the municipal albergue at the other end of town. It was absolutely freezing; I guess they couldn't keep the heating on when there was no guarantee pilgrims were going to turn up. Soon after Eva and Göran arrived the four of us walked into the village to buy food to cook for dinner. We found a *supermercado* open and chose some fish and frozen vegetables, including greens, which we hadn't eaten for ages, and some yummy chocolate for dessert. This was a novelty. We hadn't cooked on our Camino for a few reasons, one of which was I couldn't think of anything worse after those long hot days of walking. Some albergues didn't have kitchen facilities, and when there were just the two of us, it was more convenient and less exhausting to go searching for a bar/restaurant.

While the vegies thawed, we sat in a warm bar with an open fire sharing a bottle of wine and a small plate of tapas, and discovered more about each other's lives and countries. Then we headed out into the freezing night air once again, pulling our beanies down over our ears, wrapping our scarves closer to our mouths and pulling on gloves as we strolled and joked our way back to the albergue under a clear, black diamond-studded sky.

Göran cooked and joked with Mike while Eva and I set the table. I felt as though I had known this beautiful woman for a lifetime, but it had only been 36 hours. I loved her childlike playfulness, honesty and humour. I realised now what I had been missing on much of our Camino. The downside of walking this path had been the lack of human contact since we had said goodbye to Lea and Dan. This had contributed enormously to our state of mind, and, to a degree, to my injury.

We spent most of the next day walking, talking and picnicking our way to Silleda. It was quite a large town, so we decided to split up to check out the hotels: Mike and Göran went one way and Eva and I the other. This was effective and fun. It was great to just spend time with another woman. We regrouped, chose the hotel, showered, and met for dinner across the road at a restaurant called Ricardo's. I had minimal discomfort in my leg and I was feeling light of heart. All was well in our world.

The following morning we left separately, but found each other again in the next town, Bandeira. Having a town between overnight stops was a welcome treat. However, before we arrived in the town, I stepped off the road for a pit stop and got caught up in plants that I was soon to find out were stinging nettles. When we got to town, I made a beeline for the pharmacy. Catching up with Eva and Göran, my discomfort was obvious so I told my tale and we all had a great laugh over coffee and cake. After morning tea, we had time to do some window-shopping. Mike bought a wallet and I bought a couple of small gifts for family.

The four of us walked out of town together and into the beautiful lush countryside. As we were making our way up a hill, we heard a dog behind us and turned to see it hurtling our way with its teeth bared. I ran towards it shouting, my walking poles flying. Amazingly, it stopped in its tracks, turned and skulked off. Later on another dog decided it was going to have a go, but this time the farmer wasn't too far away and whistled it in. Earlier in the trip, and being a dog lover, I had given dogs the benefit of the doubt. One day as I was patting a dog that looked like a little fox terrier, Mike told me very slowly and quietly to stop patting the dog and back up. From where I was standing, I couldn't see that the dog was baring its teeth. As I started to back up, a black dog came running at us. Again, its owner, who was further down the street, yelled to the dog and it left us alone. It was the last time I stopped to say, 'Hi' to a dog in Spain.

On we walked, repeatedly climbing and descending through lush green countryside until we reached Ponte Ulla for our last sleep on the Camino. There was a strange feeling in my heart that night. I was finding it difficult to comprehend that all of this would be over tomorrow. The path had been difficult, but I didn't want it to end, not yet. It was as though I was having a dream and I wasn't ready to wake up. The thought of having to go back to my 'real' life was a little scary, and I was apprehensive about returning to my everyday responsibilities and routine.

As our little group sat around the dinner table that evening, each of us was aware of what tomorrow would bring, but our focus was on the present. We ate, drank and laughed as if we had known each other for years. Onlookers might have assumed we were long-time friends meeting for dinner to reminisce over old times. We were all very tired when we said our goodnights and agreed to walk out together the next morning.

Mike

We were only one sleep away from walking into Santiago, and my excitement was growing. That morning we walked past a handwritten sign on a fence next to an official marker pointing the way to Santiago. Someone had painted the words 'Happiness is that way' on a square of plywood with an arrow pointing in the same direction. It made me think of a picture I had seen in a guidebook. It is a famous photo of *peregrinos* on their last day of the Camino Francés looking out from a hilltop towards the Santiago de Compostela Cathedral in the distance. The walkers, with outstretched arms, are pointing to the cathedral spires – their goal is in sight. Joy and relief show on their faces. I liked this photo but there was something clichéd about it that reminded me of an old magazine advertisement or something I'd seen before. Like a 1970s billboard I remember seeing as a child in Dandenong depicting a happy family moving into a new housing estate, the picture conveys the promise of something wonderful when you finally arrive. My secret hope was that the following day we would find a similar hill and feel the same emotions as the walkers in the photo. I probably held that hope for Cici more than for myself.

On approaching our last town, Ponte Ulla, we arrived at a long stone bridge. Halfway across, the four of us stopped to witness the sun going down behind the mountains. We watched in silence as the cold blue sky became streaked with deep red. This was the last sunset we would see on the Camino. I paused to take in the moment. I felt the iciness and the stillness in the air – there was no other sound except the steady flow of the river. I thought back to the sunset of our first night, with Lea and Dan, whom we had dined with on the rooftop of the albergue in Guillena. So much had happened and now it was coming to an end.

That night we caught up with Dominik, a young German from Cologne who was doing the Camino alone. We had met him earlier in the day. He was travelling the Portuguese Way from Porto, and having finished university, he had set his sights on completing this pilgrimage before starting his first serious job. His grandfather had died earlier in the year, and Dominik had carved a walking staff from a tree from his grandfather's garden. He carried it in the style that pilgrims used before walking poles made of titanium were invented.

The five of us ate our last dinner of the Camino together that evening. In the background, locals sat at the bar watching a Real Madrid match on TV and cheering occasionally – especially when the foreign team scored against Madrid.[9] We ordered our meals in Spanish, and the waitress complimented me (*perfecto!*) when I ordered a plate of grilled sardines and by chance nailed the pronunciation. The others cheered as if I had just kicked a goal.

---

[9] We noticed that in rural Spain, there was no love lost for Madrid and this included Real Madrid.

'Sometimes I don't understand you,' said Eva, looking confused. 'You say you don't speak Spanish and then you say something like that to the waitress and you speak it better than I do!'

The dinner capped off a satisfying day and we went to bed early – tomorrow would be the last day of the Camino. As usual, we set the alarm to wake us before the sun rose. We had a fairly modest distance to cover on our last day – 22 kilometres – with no great physical challenges. We had agreed that we would aim to arrive in Santiago in the early afternoon so we could experience the feeling of being in the square in front of the cathedral during the day time and – hopefully – under sunny, clear skies.

The next morning I awoke to the sound of rain. Outside the window, the highway next to our hotel looked slick and shiny and the trucks were noisy as they drove past, making that hissing sound of tyres on wet roads. As we had done almost every day for the past 54 days, we put on our boots, checked our gear and prepared our backpacks. I was sad. This was not how I wanted it to be. I had hoped to walk into Santiago feeling the sun on my face and seeing the cathedral under a clear sky. Perhaps this was my last romantic fantasy of the Camino.

As we prepared to leave the room, we did our usual quick check that we hadn't left anything behind. I realised I didn't want to leave the room. I didn't want to walk today. I wanted to go back to bed and spend the day under the covers because I wasn't ready to end it this way – I wanted it to be perfect. But I said nothing. We left the room and walked downstairs to meet Eva, Göran and Dom for breakfast. Within a few moments, whatever I had been feeling was forgotten, washed away by the pleasure of seeing my *compadres*. We started planning the day ahead and I told myself that as wonderful as it would have been to walk into Santiago in clear weather, it was more important to walk into the city with our friends.

Throughout the morning the rain and the wind tested my 'waterproof' jacket and shoes. It didn't take long for the rain to penetrate through to my socks. Walking in wet socks had become so familiar an experience since leaving Ourense that I actually liked it. Cici, too, looked happy. For her, the rain and the cold temperatures were perfect conditions for walking. The weather didn't let up, which meant all four of us leaned into the wind as we walked, our faces shielded by the front of our hoods, which we pulled down to cover our eyes, making it hard to talk. I missed the conversations we had enjoyed in recent days and the frequent stops we had made to look at interesting things: a farmer's scarecrow, the inside of strange stilt-like structures that were commonplace on some of the properties we passed (we later discovered they were for drying corn), a particularly homely looking house or someone's lovingly tended garden.

We took a detour from the path to find a place to stop for coffee in the outer suburbs of Santiago. We had left the greenery and farms behind and arrived in the main street of a small town consisting of warehouses, a service station, a few shops and one restaurant. Climbing up the steps of the restaurant we came to a covered portico where we could leave our gear. I was cold and realised how tired I felt. Cici was in a quiet frame of mind.

Surprisingly, I hadn't seen Dominik since we'd left the hotel. He had gone back to his room as he had forgotten something. He was the fastest walker among us, and I had thought he would catch up to us in the first hour. Now that we had taken a detour, he would probably continue straight on and arrive in Santiago ahead of us – not that it had ever been a race, but I had hoped that we would all walk in together.

Inside, the four of us came to life again and we enjoyed coffee and glazed doughnuts. The waitress told us we could expect the rain to continue all day. I'm not sure why it happened, but after we had finished our coffee, we left the restaurant ahead of Eva and Göran. We were confident we would see them further down the road so we headed off without giving it a thought. Following instructions from the waitress for getting back on the trail, we set off in a new direction down the main street rather than retracing our steps.

Cici and I settled into walking in silence. As I walked, I looked mostly at my feet to shield my face. Getting back on the path was not as straightforward as we had thought and we realised it would have been quicker to double back the way we had come. We eventually found the trail and waited for a quarter of an hour for the others to catch up. After this time, we wondered whether they had chosen to retrace their steps rather than take the new route to the path.

We pushed on, thinking they were probably ahead of us. We stepped up the pace. At one point, I turned back and saw a familiar figure in the distance. Dominik was striding towards us in the rain, swinging his pilgrim's staff. We slowed our pace to allow him to catch up. He was pleased to see us and said that Eva and Göran had stopped at a bar to wait for us as they thought we might not have found the shortcut. We continued on towards Santiago, planning to stop after a while and wait for Eva and Göran to catch up.

Dominik and I walked together with Cici slightly behind, and we fell into an easy rhythm of long strides and talking. We found lots to talk about. Dom and his wife had travelled in South East Asia and the Middle East, and he would soon be starting a new job in Cologne. We charged up a hill, still talking animatedly, and when we got to the top we could see the change in the view – the denser housing and taller buildings that told us we were getting closer to the city of Santiago.

'I think we will soon smell the incense from the Catholics,' Dominik said. 'I think I can already smell it.'

'Yes, but I think you'll smell the money before you smell the incense.'

He was smart, worldly for his age, and I admired him for doing the Camino on his own. I was kind of jealous, too, that he was at the start of his career. It was all in front of him. I could remember the anxiety and excitement I had felt in my twenties when I walked out into the world full of uncertainty and hope as I tried to find my place as a young lawyer.

We reached a bridge over a railway cutting at the top of a hill. Cici soon arrived at the top and the look on her face told me two things. First, I had been an arse for powering ahead and leaving her behind. Second, while I had been having a great time chatting with Dominik, she was struggling.

'We were supposed to do this together today, remember?' she said with disappointment and annoyance in her voice. The buoyancy I had been feeling up until that point vanished.

We still hadn't heard from Eva and Göran, but in a few moments I received a text: 'Where are you both?' I told them they were definitely behind us and we would wait for them. Dominik, with his swinging staff and buoyant mood, was on a roll and decided to walk into Santiago on his own.

'It's all good! We will catch up tonight and drink lots of beer! Ciao!'

We crossed the bridge and sat down to wait for the others. Cici was still simmering. I spotted a café nearby and suggested she might want to wait in there where it would be dry and warm. I returned to the bridge to wait on my own. The sudden change of events in the last few moments made me stop and take stock of what had happened. This was not how I had thought it would be. Our little group was falling apart. The weather was shit. I felt bad for walking on and ignoring her. I was standing on a concrete overpass that crossed a railway cutting. When I first walked across, I hadn't noticed all the faded colours of objects on the railings. I returned to look more closely. People had used the tall cyclone fence on each side of the railing as a notice board, attaching messages written on coloured paper. Looking down I saw the dual tracks curve around towards the direction of Santiago and disappear at the bend. There were small houses and apartment blocks on either side of the concrete barriers separating the train line from people's homes. And apart from that, not a soul. Only silence, except for the sound of drops of rain on my hood.

The fence was covered with photos and most of these with notes attached. There were children's photos. Wives and husbands. Lots of coloured hearts and plastic flowers fading after years of carrying the memory of something terrible that had taken place here. One morning, two years ago, a high-speed train had left Santiago and had taken the bend at twice the speed considered safe for this stretch. The train had flown off the tracks and slid on its side with carriages crashing into the reinforced concrete barriers of the cutting which meant that the houses nearby were saved. However, carriages concertinaed and others became airborne, such was the great speed (estimated at 195 km/h) at which it had approached the bend. The train was full to capacity. In all, 88 people died. No one escaped injury. Many people in the local area had rushed to the scene and were first responders to the carnage and human suffering.

There were other objects tied to the fence: a child's teddy bear, a flower, a doll. This was the second worst train disaster in Spain's history. I remembered back to Granada when I lost my way looking for Cici and how I was beginning to feel emotions that had been forgotten like old clothes kept in a suitcase under the bed. Now I could feel my feelings more freely, more openly and I felt the pain in my heart for what had happened here.

I turned to see Eva and Göran appear at the other end of the bridge. The visceral shock of these images and the messages of grief now turned to relief at having found our dear friends again. Now we could complete our walk together.

Near Dozón we discovered this church open for prayer.
It offered a sanctuary from the cold and from our busy thoughts.

In the last week of our Camino, we rediscovered our joy.

Intrigued by these structures, we learned they are used to dry corn and to keep the grain safe from rodents.

Collecting fresh water from the fountain in Cea.

A statue in Cea depicting the bread for which the town is famous.

Our new-found friends Eva and Göran on an ancient Roman bridge.

One of Mike's favourite images of the Camino shows Cici, Eva and Göran walking towards Ponte Ulla.

Our last meal on the Camino (left to right): Eva, Mike, Cici, Dominik and Göran, in Ponte Ulla.

Close to our goal, our hopes were raised as we came across this sign on someone's front fence.

Arriving in Santiago
Chapter 7

Date   *1ST OCTOBER 2016*

Method of travel: (Foot) Bicycle Horse Other (Please circle)

SANTIAGO DE COMPOSTELA
COMPLETION STAMP

2 4 NOV. 2016

I'll Be Happy When

Cici

It was cold that morning and pouring with rain. It was hard to believe that it was all over except for the next 22 kilometres. Eva, Göran, Dominik, Mike and I shared breakfast together and then began to make our way up the hill on the highway that led onto a dirt road and then a muddy track. As the rain dripped off the front of my hood and my shoes squelched in the mud, I became aware of a silence within, as the mind-chatter and venting of weeks ago faded – despite the noise of the rain, the breeze, the rustling of my poncho and the clanking of the scallop shell against my pack. These noises had been with me for weeks, but seemed to become louder in the rain, reminding me of their presence.

We stopped for morning tea in an outer suburb of Santiago, looking forward to some shelter, coffee and a fresh doughnut or two (or three). After much light-hearted banter, Mike and I left first, feeling excited we were so close. We were confident that the others, being faster walkers, would catch up soon. Closer to Santiago's centre, Dominik caught up, saying that Eva and Göran had stopped at a bar about an hour back. They thought we had taken a wrong turn and were waiting there for us. We had all agreed we would walk into Santiago together, but now Dominik said he wanted to walk in on his own. Eva texted and Mike phoned her and tried to explain where we were. It was hard waiting around in the rain for around an hour while they walked to meet us.

About five kilometres ago, we had made our way to the top of a ridge and I had seen Santiago beckoning in the distance. My heart had soared as excitement radiated through me and I had felt so happy. Now, standing in the cold and rain, and being forced to wait, I spat the dummy. I was annoyed that Eva and Göran felt responsible for us, and I was peeved that I felt responsible for them. I was unsettled and upset. Mike was surprised to see me so frustrated, thinking that I didn't want to wait for our friends. Of course I did, but the waiting broke the spell of the day. We were only about an hour from the cathedral and the pleasure of anticipation had been snatched from me. My heart sank. I was weary; I was in pain from my leg; the rain wouldn't let up; we were cold and becoming colder – it felt too hard. This wasn't how my pilgrimage was supposed to end. It was a given that I expected to complete the Camino. I expected to be spiritually aware and present, and I expected to do it my way. Only much later, did I realise I had had one more expectation – to walk the last few kilometres to the cathedral slowly and reflectively, on my own.

I went to wait in a café where I calmed myself and found some balance. As I left and walked back to join Mike, Eva and Göran appeared across the bridge. It was lovely to see their sweet faces. There were apologies all round for what had happened and for any miscommunication. We took photos of each other with the cathedral spires in the background. My memory of the last few kilometres is of keeping my head down and maintaining a strong fast pace with the others as if being propelled by some unknown force uphill towards the finish line as I had done years ago in Central Park, New York. It was a blur.

I remember people in my peripheral vision, cobblestones beneath my feet, winding our way through narrow stone laneways as if walking in a maze. Then, as if having been beamed in from somewhere, we stood on the wide stone steps to the east entrance of the cathedral. It felt surreal. As I stood in a triumphant pose, my arms outstretched for the photo, I felt relieved to be there and happy that I was standing where many others had stood before me. But in that moment, something was also missing. There was a sadness creeping in, like a shadow passing across my heart, knowing the walk had ended.

We made our way around the corner to the main plaza where many pilgrims sat on the stones or lay on their backpacks taking in that they had arrived. This section of the cathedral was the main entrance but it was covered in scaffolding, which made it impossible for us to enter to visit the statue of St James. Eva asked for directions to the office where we could have our credentials stamped for the last time and receive our official certificates for having completed our journey, then we waited in line for our turn.

I sat off to the side, peering out the window. Still wearing my poncho, water dripping on the floor, I was reduced to tears that felt hot running over my cheeks. My sadness had given way to confusion that I could not articulate. Eva and Göran were in line in front of us and it was their turn to enter. On their way out, Mike took a photo of them, beaming and waving their certificates. I tried my best to meet their happiness with a smile. Mike and I entered next, each going to a different section of a long counter to be greeted by an interviewer. I heard Mike being asked, 'Why did you do this Camino?' He replied, 'I like to walk.' I burst out laughing and so did the interviewer behind the counter. This lightness helped me put today's experience in perspective.

Two certificates are presented to walkers and pilgrims, both very elegant-looking documents. Those who have walked a minimum of 100 kilometres of the Camino are presented with the 'Compostela', the cathedral's official certificate of recognition, which has been issued for hundreds of years free of charge. It states your name and the date you arrived in Santiago, but not the specific Camino walked. It is presented as an acknowledgement that the journey or pilgrimage was walked for 'religious or spiritual reasons' or with the intention of searching for meaning and purpose. The 'Certificate of Distance', a more recent document, was introduced because the pilgrims wanted to have some sort of proof of how far they walked. It also serves to raise money for the cathedral to help offset the cost of running the pilgrim office and issuing Compostelas. For this, you pay a small fee and the interviewer writes in the number of kilometres and the Camino you have walked, along with the name of the town from which you started and the date you started. For an extra few euros, you can purchase a decoratively patterned cardboard tube in which to store your scrolled certificate.

Back in the plaza, the four of us agreed we would meet there again in a couple of hours for the Pilgrims' Mass. Mike and I caught a taxi to our accommodation on the other side of town, taking in the sights to orientate ourselves as best we could in the dark through the rain-frosted windows of the car. After showering, we put our Camino gear on again as we had nothing else to wear (clothes shopping would need to wait for a couple of days) and found another taxi to take us back to the cathedral. Being in a vehicle and seeing things speed by was still quite an unsettling experience.

As I sat in the cathedral listening to the Pilgrim's Mass, my mind and my eyes wandered, taking in the fact that I had indeed arrived. I was actually sitting in this sacred place. My gaze led me to the seemingly never-ending space above me. The distance from the hallowed rafters to the unevenly spaced side chapels seemed infinite. Between the chapels nestled majestic statues of saints carved exquisitely in the stonework, a comforting spiritual presence. They peered across the rows of pews as if to deliver their own words of wisdom.

My attention returned to my immediate surroundings as people stood and sang, and then kneeled, prayed and stood again, which was the only thing familiar to me from home. The hymns and prayers reverberated against the ancient stone walls. Expectant and wondering, the sea of people sat with heads bowed, hands in prayer, arms outstretched, all aglow in the light emanating from the altar in the distance.

I could make out some of the Spanish service, especially the acknowledgement of pilgrims from countries all over the world including Australia. This information would have been gathered earlier from the official register.

I couldn't believe our good fortune when we heard the Botafumeiro was being prepared – this ritual is famous among pilgrims. The Botafumeiro is a massive silver incense burner swung from side to side within the cathedral. We moved closer to enjoy a fuller experience. *Just pinch me,* I thought. Off to the side, within the altar space, the *tiraboleiros*, whose job it is to pull on the massive ropes and generate the momentum required to swing it, were dressed in burgundy robes and stood in a circle waiting. Another *tiraboleiro*, in the centre of the altar, steadied the super-sized burner while it was being lit; it was suspended from a pulley mechanism way above. With the burner lit, the scent and smoke of frankincense began to fill the altar and the chief *tiraboleiro* gave the Botafumeiro a push to set it in motion.

Now the *tiraboleiros* pulled on the ropes, finding their timing, up and down, side to side. At first, it swings quite slowly, and then as it gathers momentum with a pendulum effect, everyone is silent, transfixed and drawn into this spiritual dance. The intensity of this extraordinary ritual was palpable, the congregation spellbound. It was as if the pendulum was spinning a cocoon of spiritual unity where, even if only for a short time, everyone present could be together in oneness.

Outside again in the cold night air, our little group silently made our way down the steps to the street. I was becoming even more conscious of where I was, and of the significance of this time and place. After all those months of planning and training, many weeks of walking, learning and growing – now it had stopped. Yet, for me, this Camino had not come to an end.

Mike

The four of us wandered through the square in the drizzling rain. It is customary, once you have completed the Camino, to visit the statue of St James. For some devout pilgrims, kneeling and kissing the feet of the statue is the climactic moment of the pilgrimage. I was curious to see what St James looked like and to witness others who would be moved by the presence of his statue.

We entered the cathedral via a side entry as the main entrance was covered in blue scaffolding for restoration work. We joined the queue so we could see the statue, only to realise there was no access to St James in the main part of the cathedral because of the renovations. As I stood there, a group of young *peregrinos* arrived. They were bubbling noisily with joy and their energy filled the cavernous space. Everything in the cathedral was totally AMAZING for them. 'Oh my God! Wow! This is incredible!' Their voices filled the quiet space.

One of them walked up to me and blurted out, 'Have you just finished today? How are you feeling?'

Before I could reply, she added, 'I feel fantastic!' and walked on. I didn't feel fantastic. I didn't know what I felt. I was numb as I moved through the cathedral with the crowd.

Cici

Eva and Göran had already completed a few Caminos and knew the town well, so Eva suggested a great restaurant where we could share a celebratory meal. We also met again the following night to celebrate Göran's seventieth birthday and to say a tearful goodbye. It was difficult to leave each other knowing we might never meet again.

It would soon be time for us to leave Santiago de Compostela as well. I had mixed feelings around this. It seemed as though I had unfinished business and I would spend many months processing my experiences.

Mike

For the first couple of days in Santiago, I would awake in the morning with that familiar sense of urgency before I remembered that I no longer had to get up, put on a pack and spend another day walking in the cold and rain. It wasn't easy after two months of being *peregrinos* to shift into new roles. We stayed in a hotel near the Santiago train station. Our packs lay unused in the corner. Our walking poles, also rested, telescoped down, in the darkness of a closet. It was a time to sleep in, to assess our injuries and find ways to reward and pamper ourselves. However, it was hard letting go of the routine that had been our lives for the past 55 days. It was as if my body didn't believe it.

Each day I tried to look forward to exploring the city. Santiago de Compostela would measure up to most people's expectations of a 'postcard beautiful' Spanish city. You can wander down numerous narrow lanes crammed with interesting little bars and discover hidden courtyards. But I was in a weird space and found it hard to appreciate the sophistication of this city. After five nights in the hotel in our comfortable beds, I wasn't sleeping restfully. I still woke at four o'clock but now I would lay there in the darkness and wonder what I was going to do today, which was not a question I had to think about on the Camino. A few times in the night I would wake up with painful 'Camino feet'. My feet seemed to think they were still on the road and I experienced what a doctor later described as phantom pains, such as cramps in the arch of my feet. Someone forgot to tell them we had stopped walking.

So what did we do in this weird in-between time? We ate tapas, hung out in the bars and cafés, and shopped for clothes. Cici visited the stylish boutiques and purchased an elegant outfit and a coat with a fur-lined hood (except she requested that they remove the fur). I bought a pair of locally hand-made shoes and some Spanish-brand jumpers that I later discovered were made in Bangladesh.

We met other *peregrinos* including a woman from London who had just completed a shorter Camino – about 240 kilometres from Porto in Portugal – and was coming to terms with what she had done. From the way she talked about her other life as a PR consultant, she sounded more like a stilettos-and-briefcase girl than a hiking-boots-and-backpack person, and I suspected the experience had been mildly traumatising for her. She needed to download to someone about it all. When she spoke, it came out like a stream of babble – perhaps we had sounded like that in the first couple of days after we arrived.

After two days, we said goodbye to Eva and Göran. It was a sad moment and we were all teary when we hugged, promising to stay in touch. Dominik had returned to Cologne to start his new job and his working life. Unfortunately, we didn't catch up with him on the night we arrived, to drink ourselves silly as promised. For some reason, our phones weren't connecting properly, so our text messages downloaded days after we had sent them.

On the third day, Marga and Jesús made contact and invited us to their home for lunch. We arrived at the front door of their apartment. Inside it was filled with antiques, a baby grand piano, lots of knick-knacks (they are both keen collectors of everything from drinking steins to historic photos) and many photos of their family, especially their son and daughter, who work in London and Madrid respectively.

Jesús and Marga greeted us warmly. We also met Marga's younger brother, Miguel, who was polite and reserved and, like her, spoke with a New York accent. They had prepared a *tarta de Santiago* for us, a traditional Santiago tart. We were touched because they didn't buy it from a *pastelería* (cake shop) but had made it themselves; they had even put our names in icing on the top.

We spoke mostly with Marga and Louis; it felt like Jesús was left out of our discussion again. He clearly wanted to know all about our journey from where they had left us at Carcaboso and he kept Marga busy translating his questions. At one point, he jumped out of his chair and moved quickly to a shelf. He brought back a small blue and white porcelain object depicting the Santiago de Compostela Cathedral. He signed and dated the bottom of it and asked us to keep it in memory of our time spent with them.

Then Cici remembered her backpack that sat in the entrance to their apartment. We had brought it because Jesús had mentioned how much he liked it. We offered it to him as a gift. He immediately put it on and marched around the apartment as if he was in some imaginary parade. Suddenly inspired, he asked whether we would like to go to the town of Finisterre on the Atlantic coast. Its name comes from Latin and means 'end of the earth'. It is a tradition after completing the Camino to burn your clothes at Cape Finisterre and begin life renewed and cleansed. Rather than walk the 100 kilometres to Finisterre, Jesús offered to take a day out and drive us. We briefly considered it, but declined the offer and the opportunity to be reborn. We knew it would be interesting and it would form another memory, but we felt we needed our downtime rather than another mini-adventure. We said goodbye and promised to return one day.

In the night, I dreamed about walking in bare feet over stone roads and woke with aching arches. I looked at the bedside clock – it was 4 am. The next morning we left Santiago. We caught a train to Madrid, unsure of how many days we would spend there. I looked forward to leaving Spain and moving on to the next part of our journey in Europe.

As we travelled on the train through Galicia, I recognised some of the towns we had walked through and the names of the stations. Many of them were small villages where our train didn't stop. A few times I glimpsed the Camino pathway wending its way through the mountains. It was a faint track but it stood out vividly to me. It seemed unreal to be speeding past these memories of only a few weeks before from the comfort of the lounge-restaurant carriage. I sat in a comfortable seat drinking coffee and thinking how my mind and body still could not accept that our adventure had ended.

Our destination became real when we saw this sign outside Padornelo.

As we walked through the suburbs of Santiago in the final hours of our journey, the spires of the cathedral came into view.

Cici arriving on the steps of the cathedral in Santiago – behind the triumphant pose are mixed feelings.

A few days after we finished our Camino, Mike returned to the square near the cathedral to take photos of *peregrinos* who had just completed their own journey.

Jesús gave us this porcelain cathedral as a gift.

A view of the spires from behind the cathedral in Santiago.

Miguel, Marga and Jesús welcoming us to Santiago de Compostela.

One way we spent our time in Santiago was enjoying the
Galician food in the many taperías.

Melbourne
Chapter 8

Lost and Found
on Home Ground

Cici

I stared out at the countryside through the window of the train heading for Madrid. My experience had definitely not been what I had imagined it would be. The road less travelled is a rocky road in every way, but I was a richer person for having taken it. The Vía de la Plata was a holistic journey, by which I mean it was an experience of the mind, body and soul. From day one, it was challenging and confronting. In the beginning, my mind had tended to want to take over, to solve everything even before it started. 'Hector' had become preoccupied with the struggle to meet primal needs, including, but not limited to, food, water and shelter. What had started out, in my very naïve mind, as a peaceful and serene pilgrimage became anything but. I did, however, experience moments of serenity and space for reflection.

In my initial struggles, I was trying to find a place where I could find some comfort in my discomfort. I wanted to dig deep knowing that all over the world, people living their everyday lives experience the hardship of heat, cold, not enough of the right food to eat, and feeling constantly vulnerable and isolated. I could pull the plug on my journey at any time but they could not. I felt humbled by this awareness. As the days turned into weeks, I found I was learning how to live in another way. It gave me a glimpse of how life is for people who are strangers in a country and where they cannot feel comfortable, safe and secure.

We received an email from Eva and Göran, who were home in Stockholm. They said they could not let us fly home to Australia without seeing us again. Some relationships are fleeting and meant to be enjoyed in the moment, but others last a lifetime. We had already planned to visit Denmark in the weeks between leaving Spain and returning to Australia, so our friends offered to meet us in Copenhagen. It was a dream coming true. I wondered whether the depth of our friendship would be evident when we sighted each other again so many weeks after the Camino.

We met in the foyer of the hotel where we had all booked to stay in Copenhagen. I was excited and a little nervous as the lift doors opened onto the reception area. We spotted one another simultaneously grinning from ear to ear. We hugged, and Eva, cupping my face in her hands, said joyously, 'It is the same, it is the same.' *Si*, it was the same. The Camino experiences we had shared had bonded us for our lifetime, just as they had with Lea and Dan. What a blessing.

When we arrived home in Melbourne mid-January 2017, everything appeared to be the same but everything had changed. I was enrolled in a course starting in a couple of weeks. There was no way I could commence this study and honour it. My heart, soul and mind were in no-woman's-land. It was as if all that had transpired was hovering in a space above me waiting for a place to settle but finding nowhere to land. Even after all these weeks I felt pressured and overwhelmed, and I was functioning like a robot much of the time. I had to trust that time would bring more clarity and that I would be guided as I gradually sifted through the overload of experiences.

Months later, Lea and Dan emailed us. They had just flown back to Spain to resume the Camino where they had left off, and they were finding their Camino legs again. They were suffering through the usual first-week complaints: aches and pains, blisters, cold sores, sunburn and so on. Mike and I looked at each other and burst out laughing at the absurdity of it. Every word of what they were willing to put themselves through resonated. The big question always remained: why?

For some inexplicable reason, some people are drawn back to the Camino again and again, and yet others cannot understand the fuss and walk away without feeling they have experienced anything profound or meaningful. As difficult as I found the walk as a novice pilgrim on that particular Camino, I don't regret a moment of it. I feel confident I will gain more insights with time and will continue to learn from the experience. It keeps me awake to life. I also know it isn't finished.

Mike

Many people who have heard of the Camino wonder if walking it changes your life. After returning to Melbourne, I sat with my bookkeeper, Dina, at the same café we had sat at six months before. She looked at me from behind her sunglasses, another latte in her hand. She had returned from her cruise around the Mediterranean and a couple of weeks in Switzerland.

'So did it?'

'What?'

'You know, change your life.'

The funny thing is it did. I replied, 'Sure, I don't like walking anymore.'

She started to laugh, spilling her coffee, and wouldn't stop, which set me off too. When we both stopped laughing (she had tears running down her cheeks), I realised that this response was the only one I could think of at the time.

In Australia, I've walked lots of overland treks – they've all given me a feeling of accomplishment and exhilaration. I didn't get that in Spain. I didn't get the high I was hoping for – especially on the last day. There was not one day when I felt that. When I went into the Camino registration office to have my credentials stamped as a peregrino, I told the official behind the counter I had done the walk because I liked walking. Now I quietly wondered whether that was still true. Maybe the Camino had wrung it out of me. Would I ever again experience the high that trekking had given me in the past? I was reluctant to find out in case the answer was 'no'.

Months later, my thoughts and moods were in a Melbourne winter funk. I was waiting for the sun and blue sky to appear and lift me out of the greyness of my muddy thoughts and feelings. This was how I felt whenever I thought about what the Camino meant for me.

One night a conversation with a stranger at dinner started to shift things for me. Our friends had invited some friends of theirs we had not met before and I was seated with one of them who asked me about the walk. In response to her many questions, I mentioned that it had been different from what I had expected.

'What did you expect?' she asked.

'What I expected was to wake up in a village, then slide out of a bed and wander down to have a breakfast of coffee and churros. Put on our packs after a restful night's sleep and walk for half the day to arrive at a charming little country village at that delightful time of the day, siesta. I expected we would then have the time to stroll around the village before finding a local restaurant where we would have dinner and enjoy a bottle of Spanish wine. I looked forward to the wonderful tapas so many people raved about. Not a bowl of potato chips. If that's what I expected, I got none of it. What did I expect? Perfection, in all its unrealistic, romantic, imagined detail. Just that! I expected perfection.'

My dinner companion continued to cross-examine me; I was surprised at how determined she was to understand why I had walked the Camino at all. I hadn't thought of the pilgrimage as being an irresponsible dalliance for a while, but now my self-doubt returned.

'So you didn't really need to do the Camino! I mean, you could have just done a lot of walks here in Australia where you could have experienced similar physical and psychological challenges without all that difficulty. You know…the inconvenience of not speaking the language…and the food. And if you were looking for some spiritual insight or some life-changing moment, you could have gone to therapy!'

I thought, *Wow, she has a point.* I also thought, *You cow, I think I hate you.*

Most of our friends had been impressed when they learned about our experience. It was flattering and I was relishing the praise from them. This evening, however, the conversation had taken an unpredictable turn. Other people at our table were tuning into our little discussion and there was a pause in which either I would respond to the woman's challenge or the diplomatic host would introduce a circuit breaker and ask everyone if they were ready for dessert. That night was one of those rare occasions when I was able to think on my feet and give a coherent response.

'Well actually, I think there is something about pushing yourself out of your comfort zone that can be valuable and life changing. And yes, I admit the Camino did not live up to my expectations, but it gave me gifts I can see only now and I would not have experienced those if I had not been out of my comfort zone. Lots of people say they like to put themselves in situations where they feel challenged, but only to a point. And while there is the possibility of having insights from going to therapy, at the end of each therapy session you go back to the familiar. You go back to your familiar little apartment, catch up with your familiar friends, eat the same familiar foods and talk about the same old things. What if you can't turn off the experience of being in unfamiliar surroundings and you can't speak the language and often cannot communicate what you need? The discomfort of that just keeps coming and the only time you can escape it is in the few hours of sleep each night. You can't change your reality – short of calling it quits and going home – so the only thing you can change is the way you think about it. I think that is how you grow as a person. That's what makes the Camino fundamentally different from therapy.'

I was conscious that I was speaking a little more animatedly than before. The host suddenly spoke up. 'Who feels like dessert? There's a divine tiramisù on the menu!' My dinner companion looked away and said nothing. I felt self-conscious for having spoken so passionately and a bit too loudly. (I later learned that she was a psychotherapist.)

Yes, I felt disappointed walking the Camino. But disappointment was just one of many emotions. It was strange and amusing after my return when some friends asked or texted me about my trek, 'Did you have fun?' 'Did you feel happy when you got to Santiago?' One even asked me, 'Was it a blast?' (Maybe he thought I had gone to Ibiza.) Yes, there were times when I felt happy. I felt happy when I was in the company of our friends, Dan and Lea and Eva and Goran. When it came to the whole experience, I felt a lot of emotions, a lot more than I had felt for many years. Happiness was not the only feeling I felt and not the most important one. When Cici and I talk about our time on the walk, we always come back to, the acts of kindness from the locals and what it felt like to be on the receiving end of that. I remember the tractor driver who invited us to help ourselves to a bunch of grapes and washed them with the contents of his water bottle; the elderly man in the tavern who showed Cici to the bathroom but didn't allow her to use it until he had cleaned and prepared it first; the generosity of Marga and Jesús. And there were lots more. Those many small gestures of hospitality and friendship stay with me because in a foreign culture where I am a stranger, the impact of those simple acts is magnified tenfold. It can be as subtle as a look, a gesture, a smile or someone taking an extra minute to point you in the right direction and explain where we can find a room to stay. I never felt estranged from people in rural Spain where people always greeted one another (and us) on the road with the words '*Buenos Dias*'. The kindness and those simple gestures are what I remember. However, the experience of feeling out of my comfort zone, and the vulnerability that goes with this is also hard to forget. I find I keep thinking of people who experience being in a similarly vulnerable position but far worse than our brief experience of discomfort. I think of people escaping some horrible situation to come to a new country and what it must be like for them. I also think of the migrant workers with little or no English whom my father felt protective of so many years ago at the plant where he worked in Dandenong. I can understand now more than ever, why he felt so strongly about giving the 'new Australians' a fair go.

That our acts of kindness can bridge distances between people is not something new, but I didn't know it viscerally until now. As I rushed to the train platform the other day, I came upon a couple of English tourists trying to buy a travel card from a vending machine. I stopped to show them how to buy their tickets even though it meant missing my train (and my appointment). My priorities melted away in that moment and I knew I had to stop to assist them. I remember how good it felt talking to them, asking them what part of England they were from and what station they needed to get to. Before leaving on the Camino, I had often read that I would be handicapped doing the Vía de la Plata if I did not have a good level of conversational Spanish. What they didn't tell me was how people's humanity could reach out to connect with you, despite not being able to converse through a common language.

I see my experience of the Camino differently now. I think how I often described it to friends as a walk, a trek or a pilgrimage. I highlighted the hardships and the challenges. I didn't see it as an adventure. In hindsight however, the Camino was an adventure – it was a grand adventure. For me, that is a puzzle that makes me smile. How did I not see it as an adventure when I was right there in it? Even in those days of heat in the high thirties with no shade, physical soreness and discomfort, and the boredom on those long flat roads across the Meseta – I look back on that now and think, *Wow, we did that. That was amazing!* It makes me wonder about the seeming ordinariness of everyday life. Can life be a grand adventure too, in all its ordinariness, frustrations and monotony? I believe so. Perhaps when we're in the middle of it, we can't quite see it.

HOSTAL VATICANO

N.I.F. 22754851-P

Plaza de España, 15 - Telf. 924 610 633

MONTERRUBIO DE LA SERENA (Badajoz)

19/03/19

Camino Mozárabe
March 2019
Chapter 9

22 - 03 - 2019

21/03/2019

6/03/2019

27-03-2

Unfinished Business

Cici

When we left Spain in 2016, we didn't want to go back any time soon. But about a year later, things changed. We had unfinished business on the Camino. In 2016, our original plan had been to walk the Camino Mozárabe, leaving from Granada to link up with the Vía de la Plata at Mérida. But as a result of time constraints, and knowing that our fitness wasn't up to it, we'd set out from Seville instead. The thought of walking another Camino brought with it some anxiety and fearfulness, but that had never stopped us before. Why would we put ourselves through it again? The answer: to do it in another way. We were both now keen to return.

The issues we had found so challenging last time – injury, heat, isolation and the language barrier – would need to be addressed. And so the planning and training began in 2018. We chose a date earlier in the year to be certain of avoiding the heat. We didn't mind the cold. We would walk only half the distance – approximately 500 kilometres, not 1,006. I would study Spanish for six months beforehand at the local community centre. On the injury front, we practised prevention. We lessened the weight in our packs (we had learned from last time); I booked regular sessions with an osteopath for my lower back and pelvis as I had been diagnosed with osteoarthritis and a mild stenosis in my lumbar region; we had our feet assessed and were fitted for orthotics. I blocked out more time for relaxation, meditation and massages, kept up my strength training at the gym with a personal trainer, and longer walks carrying our packs, first on weekends and then for longer stints with more hilly terrain to simulate the days on the Camino.

Lea and Dan in Canada, and Eva and Göran in Sweden, received our emails informing them of our plans to arrive in Granada on 1 March 2019. Lea and Dan said they had planned to be in Seville in February for an intensive Spanish course and would alter their dates so they could spend a few days with us in Granada before the start of our walk. They had already walked the Way of the Frances, the Portuguese Way and the Vía de la Plata and had not long completed another Camino, this time in France, walking from Le Puy down to the Spanish border, a distance of approximately 760 kilometres. As it turned out, they still felt good when they arrived at the border so they continued on to the Camino Del Norte for a short way, walking 940 kilometres in total. What an amazing effort.

Meanwhile, Eva and Göran, having previously walked similar Camino pilgrimages to Lea and Dan: the Frances, the Portuguese Way, Camino Del Norte, Camino Ingles and the Vía de la Plata – had returned to the Vía de la Plata to walk some of their favourite sections again – it certainly gets into your blood. They invited us to spend time with them at their home in Stockholm – it was all coming together.

Lea describes Mike and me as her 'antipodean counterparts'. Our friendship is easy-going and we enjoy, and are interested in, very similar things. With a reunion pending, we again wondered whether the relationship would still feel the same for them and for us, but when the time arrived, it was just like before and we felt completely at ease again. It was wonderful to have a big hug, to connect and to continue our bond from where we had left off a couple of years earlier. Camino magic.

After spending a few wonderful days with them in Granada, we began our Camino on 6 March. It was sad to leave our friends behind not knowing when we would see each other again. Walking out of the city I felt a little apprehensive and tried to allow whatever needed to happen just to happen. We met our first *peregrino*, David from Wales, when we arrived in Pinos Puente that afternoon, and later that afternoon we met another, Werner from Germany, with whom we shared a meal that night. David and Werner were to be our companions for most of the journey. Our Camino family was forming. And so goes the Camino.

We walked from Granada to Merida completing our 'unfinished business' on the Camino Mozarabe. We then decided to walk on to Cáceres revisiting towns we had passed through in 2016. If Ourense was Mike's favourite city, then Caceres was mine. It was wonderful to spend the next four days enjoying this city and strolling the maze of laneways before we made an impromptu decision and caught a bus to Porto (Portugal); and from Porto, a bus to Ourense. The morning after we arrived, while standing on the Ponte Vella bridge, Mike said, 'Look down at your feet.' I saw the toes of my boots lined up with a scallop shell cut into the stonework. The sight of the shell filled my heart with fondness. Mike said, 'Uh oh, what is it this time?' I grinned. I knew there was one more part of my unfinished Camino. 'Yep, I'm afraid so.' It was important to me to experience walking into Ourense because injury had prevented me from doing this on our first pilgrimage. The next morning we caught a taxi out to Xunqueira de Ambía and walked back into Ourense.

On this Camino, we were able to enjoy all the treats that Mother Earth offers in the spring time: cold nights and mornings, clear sunny days, an abundance of wildflowers including red and orange poppies, purple orchids, masses of lavender, carpets of bright yellow mustard seed and fields of young green wheat, lambs playing in the lush pastures, excited Portuguese sheep dog puppies exploring by the farm gates, and locals on afternoon strolls with no particular place to go – just enjoying being in that space at that time, perhaps meeting neighbours or ambling with their dogs.

On this Camino, we were able to enjoy walking in the mountains surrounded by breath-taking panoramic views, especially on the steep ascent to Moclín on the second day. It filled me to the brim with gratitude, surrounded by nature. It was also a wonderful distraction from the steady uphill climb. The hilly climbs were to be a feature of the next ten days, but we preferred them rather than the flat constant grind of the Meseta on the Vía de la Plata.

On this Camino, we were able to enjoy life without the blistering heat – to snuggle up in a warm bed on an icy night. To walk feeling relaxed instead of anxious, free from the overwhelming heat that had depleted our energy. We circled around huge puddles of water and overflowing streams instead of crossing parched, cracked earth. We felt surrounded by life in its natural flow that provided a strong sense of nurturing.

On this Camino, we were able to enjoy walking free of pain and injury.

In 2016, I had felt 'called' to the Camino, but by the end I found I was 'driven'. In 2019, I felt more 'drawn' to complete the route we had originally planned. It was two very different Caminos, walked by two different me's. In 2019, I struggled with the fact that I didn't keep a journal of my journey as I had painstakingly done the first time. My self-talk said, 'But you won't remember.' *No,* I thought, *just let it go and be present to the experience.* I didn't receive a blessing like the one I had sought out in Seville before the first pilgrimage either. In my mind, I labelled this second Camino 'unfinished business'. Maybe I thought I was still on the first Camino so I didn't need a new blessing (the first one had not yet expired).

Each day I waited for the time when I would feel connected in the same way I had felt spiritually connected on the first Camino. I felt it when climbing into Moclín, but in the following days, when we walked through a few large cities in a row, I felt distanced again. We hadn't experienced so much city life on the Vía de la Plata, especially so soon in the walk. As lovely and as historically significant as these places were, they were a constant distraction from what I perceived as my pilgrimage. The busyness, tourism, people and traffic required my energy to cope with them, and at the same time, I felt the need to change my focus and become a tourist to appreciate what each city had to offer. I was confused and torn. It wasn't until we reached Ourense in Galicia that I reconnected, and again on the outskirts of Santiago de Compostela. Had my sense of spirituality, or my perspective of it, changed? I was conscious of self-compassion and self-care being more important for me on this second pilgrimage.

In Córdoba, I took time out to visit the Caliphal Baths, a hammam, in the tradition of the Moorish bathhouses, where I luxuriated in the bath and received a massage. I would not have contemplated doing something like this on the 2016 Camino. The 'me', whom I thought needed to change, had changed. The 2019 pilgrimage taught me to surrender my driven-ness, not only on the Camino but in my personal life as well. It was finally time to let go.

Mike

When we returned to Granada in 2019, my memories of our experiences on our first Camino were clear and vivid. I wanted to experience that again, but I wanted to be more present in the moment this time. Since returning in early 2017, I no longer enjoyed long walks and I missed that. I missed the thrill of putting on my walking boots and heading down a country road. I missed the excitement and curiosity that goes with not knowing what lies ahead – 'I wonder what's around the next corner? I wonder what will be in the next town?' I guess I hoped that it would feel more like an adventure this time.

Some people assumed, again, that I would be taking another holiday in Spain (as if the first Camino had been a holiday). No. This would be a trek, a pilgrimage, a hike, but not a holiday. I hoped to revisit some towns that I had been in a rush to leave or had not wanted to slow down and explore the first time

– places like Alcuéscar, the town of the monastery where the bed broke. I hadn't cared to look around the first time; we had just wanted to get to a doctor in the next large town.

Not having had any clear motivations in 2016, I was now clear on what I wanted to experience and what I didn't. I wanted to discover new parts of rural Spain. I didn't want to walk the old routes again, but I did want to revisit some cities that I had fond memories of, like Mérida, Cáceres, and my favourite, Ourense.

I had always regretted the last day of the walk into Santiago in the rain, which made the whole experience a touch bleak. But I didn't want to get too excited at the idea of a second chance because what if it rained again? Galicia is known for its high rainfall. What I didn't want to experience was the injury and suffering. Unlike Cici, I didn't regard suffering as an unfortunate, but required, part of the walk. She was doing a spiritual pilgrimage and that was her concept of what a pilgrimage is all about. Hardship is okay. I can do hardship, but suffering and injury are different.

I knew that we had learned lots from our last trek. For one, we knew how to pack more efficiently, which meant we could keep the weight down and save our backs, and in Cici's case her leg, from injury. There were some challenges that would be new for us, such as walking into the mountains where there would be the chance of snow and the closure of some albergues over the colder months. But we wouldn't know until a few days before we were due to arrive. We had heard stories of the route requiring some river crossings and also some alarming stories of pilgrims who waded across rivers balancing their packs above their heads (along with their trousers and boots) with the water at thigh level.

Just before we left, I had a brainstorming session with some friends over many beers. They offered creative but useless tips like taking a flying fox and a crossbow to shoot the line across the river. In the end, Cici and I talked about the level of risk we were each comfortable with. We knew that the physical risks we faced this time would be different because we would be in Spain in the early spring. We would not face the baking heat and the long dry plains but instead, there would be rivers (including fast flowing ones) to cross. In the end, we decided that we would not wade through them even if this meant finding a much longer way around so as not to risk cutting our feet, twisting an ankle or losing our gear in the waters. There were other risks too, such as sudden drops in temperature and even snow in the mountains. We decided we would face those challenges as we found out more information closer to the time. Unlike last time, I didn't have any fears about leaving my business. I knew I could rely on a very dependable colleague to keep things running while I was away. This time I just knew – call it faith – that whatever happened, the business would be okay, I would be okay.

We were away for ten weeks: five weeks of those on the Camino, including one detour via bus to Porto in Portugal. I have now been back for three months and the memories are still vivid, but probably not as vivid as those of the 2016 walk. The heat and the hardship of 2016 had burned itself deep into my memory. The 2019 Camino was a rich experience, but a lighter, more joyous one. We were blessed by the change in the seasons that meant cooler, more pleasant conditions to walk in. And we were blessed by new friendships and old friendships rekindled, and again the companionship of curious, friendly animals along the way. My appreciation of these farm animals helped me to decide that I would become vegetarian, which I did after the 2019 walk.

I rediscovered the bond that is the Camino sisterhood and brotherhood – the bonds of connection and affection that so quickly form and seem to endure between *peregrinos*. We were touched that Dan and Lea made the trip from Seville to Granada to visit us. Lea had broken her ankle in Seville and was in a wheelchair. It was a sad moment when we started our Camino from the steps of the cathedral and walked off leaving them behind, knowing we could not share this adventure with them as we had shared so much of the 2016 Camino.

There is something that breaks down barriers between *peregrinos* and we experienced it again – it was not just a fluke with Lea and Dan, and Eva and Göran. We experienced something similar with David from Wales and Werner from Hamburg, and later with David's friend Bill when we all caught up for a wonderful dinner and celebrated Cici's birthday in Mérida (where Bill's and David's humour kept us laughing all night).

I found more moments of joy in the 2019 Camino because I was more present – yes, actually present – to my surroundings. There were many such moments including walking into Mérida and seeing fields of poppies and wheat bending and moving in the wind like a Mexican wave; the beautiful colours at the end of the day as we walked into Cáceres for the first time heading westwards towards the setting sun (we hadn't walked into it last time because of injuries and exhaustion); and the walk into Santiago on a delightfully sunny day, with the memory of our friends from the last Camino, Eva, Göran and Dominik, walking with us.

In the last few hours as we came into view of the cathedral spires of Santiago, we were both overcome with emotion and had to sit on a low stonewall. I remembered that Eva and Göran had taken a photo of us near this spot in the rain those years ago. The sun was streaming down on us now. A small family group were walking past. I leaped up and asked one of them if he would take our photo with my phone. He happily obliged and we introduced ourselves. I don't know if it was the look on our faces or the significance of the moment they sensed, but they seemed to linger to share this moment with us. I took a picture of them – all of them striking a happy pose with waving hands and broad smiles. After they left, I looked down at the photo he had taken of us. We were both beaming. I looked over at Cici whose tears flowed as she looked at the spires in the distance. I kept thinking, what an adventure! I can't believe it! I never thought we would return.

And yes, I rediscovered my love of walking.

Before commencing the Camino, we wined and dined in Granada with our compadres, Lea and Dan.

Having left our starting point at the cathedral we are full of quiet excitement as we walk through the empty streets of Granada in the early morning.

Ready to leave from the front of the cathedral to embark on the first day of the Camino.

Leaving the streets and suburbs of Granada behind,
we were finally in the open country.

Relaxing at dinner with our (2019) Camino family in Alcalá La Real after a hard day's
walk (L to R: David, Mike, Cici and Werner).

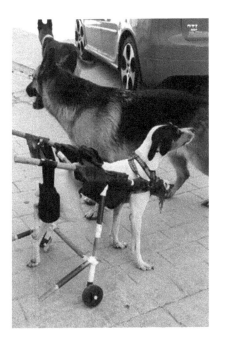

Unlike many of the sad images of dogs we recall in 2016, this time we hear the heart-warming story of 'Lucky' who was rescued by his current owner after a severe beating that left him with a broken back.

Arriving at the albergue in Moclin after a long steep climb.

Camino markers took many different forms.

The steep climb into Moclín.

Climbing up to Mocíin looking back to the town of Olivares.

A view of the town from the fourteenth-century Moclín castle.

The path to Alcuéscar was lined with spring wildflowers.

We took off our packs to take a
break under one of the holm oaks.

Lush fields of wheat – so
different from 2016.

Walking towards Ourense

Alfonso de Fonseca (1475–1534). He was archbishop of Santiago de Compostela from 1507. His reflective pose mirrored what we were both going through after arriving in Santiago.

Arriving in Alcalá la Real.

Traditional Roman baths in the centre of Ourense.

Returning to the spot where in 2016 we viewed the spires of Santiago Cathedral in the rain.

Santiago Cathedral.

Walking into Mérida at the end of the day.

A birthday celebration in Merida with David and Bill

Appendix: Practical Tips

Packing List

Most people start out carrying far more clothing and equipment than they need, and Mike and I were no exception: on the Vía de la Plata, Mike's pack weighed 15 kilograms, mine 12. Over the next few weeks we posted items home in batches (or gave them away) until we were down to the bare essentials and about half the original weight. We walked in the same pair of trousers and long-sleeved shirt every day for two months. The trousers zipped off to become long shorts.

By the time we reached Santiago de Compostela, we were carrying or wearing only the following items:

- Documents: travel documents, passports, pilgrim credentials, wallets, map guidebook (we tore out the pages we had used each day so it became lighter as we went)
- Mobile phone and iPad
- Swiss Army knife
- Journal (Cici)
- First-aid kit: scissors, saline, Band-Aids, Betadine, razor blades, gauze, moleskin, Micropore tape, pieces of fleece, eye drops, Imodium, Panadol, antibiotics (most of these can be bought along the way; rural Spain has no shortages of pharmacies)
- Sunglasses
- Toiletries: moisturiser, 3B anti-chafing cream, lip balm, sunscreen,
- toothbrushes, toothpaste, toilet roll, tissues
- Water bottles (one-litre stainless steel bottles each)
- Underpants (two pairs each) and socks (three pairs each)
- Crop top (Cici)
- Short-sleeved thermal top (one each)
- Long-sleeved thermal top (one each)

- Long-legged thermals (one each)
- Spare shirt to wear in town after we had showered
- Buff (neck protection)
- Waterproof gloves
- Poncho (Cici)
- Raincoat (Mike)
- Hat
- Head torches
- Walking poles

Non-Essential Items

We posted several parcels home as we off-loaded items we didn't really need. We also left things for other people to use: at the Airbnb in Granada I left a book on Spain and Mike left a biography of Barack Obama, a weather proof jacket for Andy, a small Bluetooth keyboard (I don't know what he was thinking bringing it along). I gave away a guidebook by Alison Raju (it was a precious gift but too heavy to carry or post), and I left a pair of sandals at an albergue in Casar de Cáceres, which I swapped for a pair of shorts. Mike gave a Bluetooth speaker to a cyclist at the same albergue. I left my heavy boots on a park bench in Zafra.

We posted parcels home on five occasions:

- Sleeping bags
- Inflatable mattresses
- Inflatable pillows
- Collapsible bowls
- Camping forks and spoons
- Keen walking boots
- Extra short-sleeved thermal top
- Extra long-sleeved thermal top
- Extra socks and underwear
- Extra crop top
- Extra shirts
- Leather hat
- Mike's Leatherman tool

- Two water bottles
- Small shoulder bag
- Small gifts for family and friends

Foot care (Cici)

Before leaving home, I asked my podiatrist to make up a first-aid kit for my feet (see the packing list earlier). The podiatrist also instructed me on how to care for and treat my feet when they became blistered, chafed and strained. This helped enormously. However, friction and dehydration will play a big part in damaging your feet during long-distance walking no matter what shoes or boots you have chosen to wear.

I started out walking in Keen boots, but boots didn't work for me – they were too hot and heavy. After about a week, I left them on a park bench hoping someone would be use them. From the beginning, I also carried Merrell walking shoes, and I wore these until around the 800-kilometre mark when the left shoe started falling apart, which was causing me pain because it no longer provided support. I replaced them with a pair of shoes I bought in Ourense and walked the last 100 kilometres in those. I expected to experience problems with them because they weren't worn in, but nothing eventuated. More than a year later I still had those Salomons.

Listen to other people's experiences and take from them what you feel may work for you. Our Spanish friends, Marga and Jesús, rubbed Vaseline into their feet each morning and walked in trail sandals over thin cotton socks and didn't experience any trouble with their feet. They only carried daypacks, which may have made a difference.

I began a little ritual with my feet a couple of hundred kilometres into the walk. Each day after arriving in a town, I had a shower and massaged my feet. Marga impressed upon me the importance of hydrating the feet before going to bed. I applied hydrating gel oil I found in pharmacies in Spain under the brand ISDIN Foot Care (it is unavailable in Australian pharmacies). Each morning I dressed any blisters and massaged the gel oil into my feet again. I wore a pair of thin moisture-wicking socks over the gel oil, and then wore a second pair of medium-weight walking socks. With this morning-and-night routine, I didn't have any more problems with my feet. Back in Australia, I buy the gel oil online, but the postage is a little expensive, so when I run out good old Vaseline is my backup.

After completing the Camino, having walked every day for so long, we experienced 'Camino syndrome'. I found I was very restless at night. I dreamt that I was putting on my pack, adjusting my straps, and then I would wake to feel my legs moving in bed as if still walking on the path. Have you have ever seen dogs paddling in their sleep?

Also, not only straight after the Camino but even when we arrived back in Australia for quite some time, we experienced what we called 'Camino feet'. When we hopped out of bed in the morning and tried to walk, our feet felt arthritic, as if they couldn't flatten or were curled at the edges. It was probably the body in automatic response mode saying, 'No, no, no. No more.'

I need to say here that given what I asked of my body I am eternally grateful for its resilience. In times of pain and injury, when the last thing on my mind was taking rest days, I was conscious that I wouldn't be going anywhere if I didn't look after my earthly outer shell. Stretching, massage, hydration, kindness and rest all go a long way to supporting and caring for yourself.

Accommodation (Mike)

Many friends and family who have learned about our walk assumed that walking the Camino meant staying in hotels, Airbnb's or hostels. But as pilgrims, who were armed with our Camino passport credentials, we had the option of staying in albergues – pilgrim accommodation. We spent most nights in this type of accommodation, and the standards varied a lot. Albergues range from very basic to unexpectedly well appointed, like the one we stayed at in Baños de Montemayor. Most have segregated bunk-style accommodation, a shared kitchen and eating area, and shared bathrooms. Often albergue owner-managers rely on the donations of pilgrims to keep their doors open and are managed by volunteers from the local community. Some rely on support from the local government, which subsidises the costs of running them.

A few of the albergues were particularly memorable for me because they had once been someone's home and still had a homely feel about them. The original owners may have been sympathetic towards pilgrims and offered a room and a meal in the spirit of hospitality, often in exchange for a donation or a fee. Sometimes when the owners died, it was their wish that their home continue to provide a night's lodging to pilgrims. These homes became albergues and are now operated by the original owners' children or, in some cases, the local government authority. Some albergues featured a photo of the original owner in the vestibule or living room next to a framed prayer or benediction for the pilgrim traveller and a donation box. It never felt that the albergues were run as businesses and that we were merely paying visitors.

Language (Cici)

It is advisable to have a decent level of conversational Spanish to make life easier on the Camino Vía de la Plata. In 2016, I had enrolled in a Spanish class a few months before leaving Melbourne, but the course was cancelled, so my only lessons came from listening to some CDs in the car for a few weeks as I travelled to and from work. My tip would be to find a course at least six months before you plan on leaving as I did in 2018. I felt so much more confident, and I was understood much more than I was on my first Camino.